F

# The Key to a Thriving Classroom

Kelly Almer

[ME] Pub

Cover image: Adobe Stock Images
Cover design: Joseph R. Myers
Layout: Marilee Pankratz

ISBN 978-1-7334334-2-6

Printed in the United States of America

To Mark: for your enduring support. You always believed in me and the gift I had for teaching that I sometimes couldn't see in myself. You helped me reach inside to bring to the surface everything I had in me to help shape future lives day in and day out in my classroom.

To Caitlin and Steven: As you both grew up, seeing my work and the value of education through your eyes brought inspiration to me to give the best of myself for our current and future generations. It is this passion for life and learning that I hold onto, cherish, and want to instill in educators everywhere.

For additional information and resources
scan the QR Code above.

# TABLE OF CONTENTS

# FOREWORD

The hallmark of my career can be summarized in one concept: Education is always about the student. However, to achieve student-centric education you must support teachers with creative, alternative, and flexible tools that are aligned to rigorous standards. Teachers need encouragement and freedom to do the job they are called to do. FLEX-ED is a wonderful story and resource that seeks to give real-world examples and tools so that teachers can create instructionally sound learning environments to provide high quality instruction.

Over the years, I've seen too many teachers exit their positions because they feel stifled and burned-out. Those of us who are no longer in the classroom seem to have the ability to exhaust enthusiastic teachers with requirements that have little to do with student-centric education. FLEX-ED is a hopeful tool that promotes teacher creativity and shows how student-centric learning can still be accomplished in the mire of administrative requirements.

Every principal should give this book to their new teachers and to those who are becoming disillusioned before it's too late. Students need teachers at their best. Teachers need the best resources. FLEX-ED is just such a resource.

–Dr. Jesus Jara
Superintendent, Clark County School District

## PREFACE: WHY FLEX-ED?

Historically, education was more organic than organizational. Learning happened at home and in people's lived environments. But over time, teaching our future leaders has become more institutionalized and...*inflexible*. Rules and requirements have multiplied. Test scores have become paramount to the success of schools, to the detriment of many students. Educators placed desks in grids across classroom floors; teachers spoke, and students listened and wrote, but curiosity did not thrive. Education grew more inflexible in policy, personnel, and furnishings.

But just as offices and workplaces have moved toward flexible environments over the past fifty years, I and other teachers and administrators have seen that education must also adapt. By prioritizing more flexible atmospheres and practices in education, we will better engage our students, stoke their curiosity, and remain inspired in our own roles as educators.

–Kelly Almer

# CHAPTER 1

# THE MISSING PIECE

One afternoon in August, just as my final year of teaching was beginning, a dear friend (and one of my former assistant principals) asked me why I was leaving education. She wasn't only wondering why I was leaving. She also didn't understand how I was still so positive after thirty-three years of teaching. How could I be walking away with my joy and vision unimpaired? I wasn't leaving on a stretcher. What was my secret?

Although her question took me by surprise, I needed no time to think of an answer. I approached every August of my career with the intent to embrace whatever the "new" would bring: new curriculum, teammates, literature, and direction. Yes, I know, our comfort zones tell us all the new stuff is stupid. Systems can make us cranky, myself included. It seemed that every year the river of "new" overflowed its banks and threatened to turn the teaching life into a bog.

But I approached those times as opportunities. My secret was simple: *I knew I had to remain teachable.* The moment I settled into obstinate attitudes, I would effectively be finished as a servant of knowledge and students. So, every August I looked for the golden nugget, maybe two, that I could use immediately to help my students (and myself). Education, like students, is fluid, never static. Teachers who think things can be simple and stationary, with nothing new added to their plate, will never realize the potential that's lying right in front of them. I remained teachable. When "new" presented itself, I learned to climb the mountains of work, to embrace the demands, to examine my usual methods through a different lens.

In doing so, I gained new freedom. I embraced the idea that I was the first and primary person who must remain teachable. Just as I asked and expected my students to cultivate a flexible attitude, I, like every teacher, needed to do the same. I needed to develop true resilience—the ability to bounce forward, not just *back*, from every "new" teaching trick, concept, or system. I discovered that supple and buoyant thinking brings growth.

I also learned that educators need a Hippocratic oath:

### FIRST, DO NO HARM.

If administrators and teachers continually gazed at those words on the wall, maybe they would better think through the actions and reactions of each day's work. What if, like doctors, educators started with the simple but transformative oath to just not hurt anyone today? What if each teacher habitually asked, *What value did I bring to my room today? Who and what did I support? Did I leave the space and my students better than when I first walked in?*

Would that help us better see the possibilities in our students, our world, and our future? What if we coupled the wisdom of that oath with a commitment to remain teachable? I think the reason I finished my career with my full love of teaching intact was that I tried to approach each day by remaining open to all the possibilities it would bring. I had resolved to do no harm, and I had resolved to remain teachable and flexible. And mental pliability precedes organizational flexibility.

It also helps that I think I always knew district personnel and administrators had everyone's best interests at heart. No matter what inservice training or new curriculum brought each year, there was sound research behind it. In learning to trust this, my flexible attitude kept me open to discovering ways to incorporate the new into my routines and rhythms. I wanted to better my craft and therefore help my students grow and improve.

### LIFE IS WHAT HAPPENS
### WHILE WE'RE MAKING OTHER PLANS.
#### -John Lennon-

As a first-year teacher, I was consumed with creating lesson plans, making seating charts, and developing cute bulletin boards. My educational training did not teach me to listen to students. And it certainly did not train me to be flexible with them or to design a flexible classroom. I approached education as a paint-by-the-numbers vocation.

That changed January 28, 1986.

I was teaching my sixth graders about paragraph building when the space shuttle Challenger blasted off. The crew included America's first teacher in space, Christa McAuliffe, who had been chosen from thousands of applicants to the NASA Teacher in Space Project. I had considered applying for that position myself, and was thrilled that NASA had filled the spot with a fellow teacher. We could not watch that historic launch at school that day, but every teacher was galvanized because "one of us" was lifting off the pad and headed for space. Minutes later, a school administrator came into my room, pulled me to the side, and told me Challenger had exploded seventy-three seconds into its flight. There were no survivors.

I had to continue teaching, saying nothing of what happened until the office gave us a statement to read to the students. I read it to my class word for word. Although we were all in shock, I had no script for discussing what had happened. So we didn't.

The following day we didn't talk much about it either, despite some students reaching out to me for help in understanding what had happened. I was at a loss as much as they were. They needed guidance, a way to process such a massive national tragedy. They knew a teacher had died in the explosion, and they knew I was a teacher. That gave my students a human reference point. But as a teacher, my job was to move forward with the curriculum.

I wanted to flex, to step out of the plan I'd made for teaching, but I had no direction or permission for reaching out as an adult to the younger humans in the room and in my heart. That's when I first realized that something crucial to our humanity might be missing in K-12 education. We didn't seem to know how to flex into honest and human responses. As America faced a whole series of tragedies over the coming years—the HIV/AIDS epidemic, 9/11, Hurricane Katrina, the Columbine school shooting, and other school shootings—that incapacity became more pronounced and disabling. I probably felt it more deeply in my career, family, and friendship circles because we lived so close to the Colorado school shootings.

As a teacher, I've had to write reports of child abuse to social services. I've practiced tornado and lockdown drills. In protecting myself and one of my students from an angry parent, I've become the target of a lockdown. I have taken other, sometimes drastic, steps to protect my students from any potential harm. I and most other educators know about the many and serious life interruptions that impact the classroom.

I also know how personal tragedy has impacted my teaching life. I sat by my husband's side in the ICU when he was critically injured in a bicycling accident. Even under those circumstances

I wrote lesson plans day after day while our family's life was turned upside down. As I sat by his side for days in the hospital, I wondered how many other professions asked so much of their employees when crises and tragedies struck. Was my hard work the result of pure dedication to my job and my students? Did it indicate a fear that I could lose my job? Did I think they couldn't get along without my detailed plans?

Don't misunderstand. I always loved teaching; it was a wonderful career. My students and I often melted down in laughter. I know the thrill of seeing students suddenly "wake up" to a new way of seeing a math problem or the world. But, looking back, I see that the crises, the catastrophes, and the broken hearts deepen us more than the silly times. They push our humanity past academic acumen. They take us deeper into emotional intelligence. We all gain something irreplaceable through the most difficult experiences. Throughout my husband's accident and recovery, I and our two children learned what really matters. And I have carried what I learned to this day. That year my students also proved that they were resilient and resourceful despite the upheaval. I learned to give them more credit than I had ever imagined possible.

People—regardless of roles, ages, special needs, or other "boxes"—have great value and need to be heard. Through my life and my experiences in education I have learned to respect every voice. My students have taught me as much or more than I have taught them. Together, we all emerged stronger through the bad days and still loved each other.

Over the years I've learned how to acknowledge more of our humanity in the classroom. I've mourned the loss of some of my students, gone too soon, leaving their families in heartbreak. And in those times, I saw them more clearly as who they were as humans, not just as students. Those losses and heartbreaks awakened in me the need to let all students know they are seen and valued and appreciated. No one is unimportant.

I've also been privileged to see former students go on to greatness; it humbled me to share their shining moments. A former elementary student became a famous opera star, another a published author, and another a renowned doctor working to find a cure for COVID. One student became a prominent aerospace engineer. What an honor to be part of a profession where I could engage so many lives.

In all of this, I have often recalled railroad crossing wisdom, "Stop, Look, and Listen." What students say or don't say reveals so much about what is happening below the surface. There have been moments when I learned I had to lay the curriculum and my lesson plans aside. At times I've had to reach deeper in order to make a small difference in a life that needed more. Whether it's due to a pandemic, a space shuttle explosion, or something as simple as a student marking the loss of a first lost tooth, celebrating the birth of a baby sister, or witnessing a wedding in a family, life's emotional moments need to be addressed. They make us stronger. They enable us to connect to colleagues, family, and friends.

I've also embraced the truth that students should have the freedom to seek answers to the real-world questions and dilemmas they face. Our life-changing moments create the vulnerabilities that open us to real learning, to relying on the collective strengths and passions of the community. After the Challenger explosion, I began to see that I could no longer afford to contain students' education strictly within the confines of the curriculum. I needed to let them cope with real life, launching their inquiring minds.

I've discovered within myself and my students a need for more flexibility and sensitivity to not just our academic needs, but to our emotional needs. FLEX-ED describes a state of mind, one that is essential to the continuous training of our younger members.

That is why I wrote this book. This is my story, and it's also a story for fellow educators who are looking for ways to continue learning and continue being inspired—and continue inspiring their students. The stories and ideas here are meant to be taken back to your own classrooms and applied in your unique environments. It is my hope that they will help you in your own journey through FLEX-ED.

# CHAPTER 2

# FISH TANKS AND HOT-AIR BALLOONS

Imagine walking into a classroom containing a couple of large saltwater tanks. You hear the low gurgle of aeration, and you see data-gathering stations clustered around them. Some students are creating videos about sea life; others plot data of the water temperatures, nitrate, and nitrite levels. Others work to solve problems before fish start dying. You see a continual buzz of activity around podcasting stations and publishing stations. Some students track and gather data about the eels' habits and movement. What a creative learning space!

When the janitors turned off the school lights for the summer break, the only glow came from those two seventy-five-gallon fish tanks in a sixth-grade classroom. The "dry tank" contained amphibians, while the wet tank was home to saltwater fish. Centrally located in the classroom, student desks and chairs fanned out around the tanks, arrayed like small science laboratories.

Even with staff gone for the summer, the fish tanks would remain on; the custodians would service them throughout the vacation.

Easy enough.

But one afternoon, an overhead tank light fell into the water. Smoke drifted up from the tanks and quickly filled the room. The fire alarm system called the local fire department. Thankfully, nothing ignited. The tanks survived. The inhabitants, unfortunately, did not. But the teacher had to relocate the classroom to the cafeteria until the mess was cleaned up.

## How I Learned to Look at Life Through My Students' Eyes

Several months later, when the classroom was deemed habitable, the room reverted to the traditional learning mode. No more science laboratories or hands-on learning. As I considered that change through student eyes, I realized the school had missed an opportunity to demonstrate resilience and mastery for the students. When setbacks or disasters come to real life, most people work to overcome them. I wondered: *Did we give up too easily? Why didn't we push through to bring the same innovative and invigorating structure back to that classroom? Why didn't we continue to let students learn all about water biomes, discuss the mishap, and explore how we could improve the tanks to prevent the same mistake in the future?*

As educators, don't we want our students to figure out what worked (or didn't) and why? Don't we want them to fight for success? The fish tank fiasco could have provided students with an authentic problem to solve. It now stands in my mind as another of many missed learning opportunities. It is also another example of how our approach to learning has not changed as much as necessary.

Because of the fish tank episode, in my third year of teaching I began assisting my school's marine biology club. Instead of two tanks, we placed thirteen saltwater tanks, ranging from fifteen to 150 gallons, throughout the building. All required consistent and vigilant maintenance.

Few things were more rewarding to me than seeing students master a siphon pump. The student would place one end of a long clear tube in the poop-filled gravel at the bottom of the tank, and the other end of the tube in his or her mouth. When they sucked, the fish poop water rushed into the tube. They quickly learned to drop that end of the tube into a plastic bucket, without getting a mouthful of the gunk. Incredibly, the students loved that job. Thankfully, no one became ill, and the fish tanks were the school's pride and joy.

Of the thirteen tanks, the eel tank drew the greatest student participation. The eels loved to play hide and seek with whoever cleaned the rocks and glass. They would slip into the filtration tube at one end of the tank, swim under the base filter, and pop up through the tube at the other end to bite any hand in the water. That required one student to watch the tank, letting their cleaning partner know whenever an eel slipped into the filtration tube. That student would quickly clean inside the tank and start siphoning the water before getting nibbled.

I discovered over and over that authentic learning—like caring for the living things in the tanks—engages real life. Authentic learning reaches students at their "interest entry points." They prefer that highly engaging, saturated learning space. Everything we did in our marine biology club gave students opportunities to engage in genuine how-the-world-works jobs and projects. And they all led into deeply reasoned changes of mind. Including mine.

⚙ **TEACHER TIP:**
Consider adding a fish tank to your room. It need not be a large one. A fifteen-gallon freshwater tank would serve the purpose—introducing another species to spark students' interest in something beyond themselves.

## Hot-Air Balloons

A few years later, while teaching at a different school in the same district, I encountered another real-life adventure with this type of learning: hot-air balloons and Sterno cans.

My teammate and I taught a unit on measurement to our students. Finding the material to be distinctly lacking in excitement, we introduced an aeronautical element in the form of tissue paper hot-air balloons. The construction of those floating creations required measurement, math, and large scoops of creative expression. However, the classroom environment did not reflect or facilitate our enthusiasm for that activity.

So, we decided we didn't need the students' desks for hands-on learning. We needed a production floor, a large area for measuring, drawing, cutting, and gluing. After giving the students materials, templates, and rudimentary instructions for balloons, we turned them loose to figure out the rest for themselves. And they did! They produced three-foot-high balloons, reflecting varying levels of craftsmanship. The results were clear: They had unknowingly used their math skills to create works of art.

We invited parents and students to join us on the playground before school one morning. Like Kennedy Space Center launch spectators, we would watch the students launch their aeronautical creations. One by one, students handed us their balloons. We carefully placed each over a Sterno flame. Would the heat make them airborne that chilly morning? Most lifted gently into the air and floated six to eight feet high as the students chased them across the playground. Catching the sunlight, they looked like holiday lights floating across the schoolyard.

The last balloon had been constructed with great gobs of Elmer's glue and many sheets of tissue paper, making it the heaviest.

Although that team didn't take its weight into consideration, we didn't have the heart to stop them. So, we gently placed it above the Sterno flame. What could go wrong?

As soon as it lifted off, a gentle breeze blew the flames up into the balloon. In a matter of seconds, it burst into a flaming replica of the Hindenburg in the morning sky. When we hit it with our fire extinguisher, it crumbled to the ground in a mess of white foam and ashes. My teaching partner and I froze, expecting a roar of disappointment. Instead, we heard,

"Cool!"
"Awesome!"
"Do it again!"

Allowing kids to decide where they want to go with a learning project allows them the chance to do things they (and we!) never imagined were possible. What we thought was going to be a disappointing crash-and-burn project morphed into a lesson about heat, air pressure, weight, and better ways to launch into flight!

Reflecting further on that event, I saw that my aeronauts and I could have modified our environment to replicate a hot-air balloon factory. Various flying machines and lighter-than-air objects could have hung from our ceiling as examples of aviation successes. It would have been easy to add other curricular topics to the math lessons for an integrated learning unit. This reminded me of something important: Teachers can find purposeful reflection that leads to deeper learning, both during and after the unit.

**☼ TEACHER TIP:**
Consider adding one construction element to a unit you are teaching. Bring supplies from home, such as toilet paper rolls, string, toothpicks, or yarn. Have them handy for unique demonstrations of any topic.

## New Shapes and Sounds

We've all seen classrooms full of students working, facing forward, answering questions, taking notes, and turning in papers. But is that really the best way to learn? Do we need to dig deeper? Can we change the learning environment? When I looked at my young students with their hot-air balloons, when I saw their joy as they worked all over the floor instead of at their desks, I began to question the way we taught. Then, caught in the grip of my own questions, I learned to change my mind.

Changing minds may not be in teacher job descriptions, but it is an essential role. The future demands it.

For example, throughout most of 2020 and much of 2021, our world coped with a global pandemic. Educators were asked to teach in various situations: online, hybrid, or with dual learning (both in-person and on-screen) simultaneously. Social distancing does not support group dynamics. Now, as teachers return to classrooms, they are pivoting their rooms from flexible learning environments to a combination of traditional rows of desks and tables with flexible seating to keep children safe. One public high school teacher told me recently that because of social distancing, her students don't know the other student two desks away. Collaboration went out the window as the virus came into our learning structures.

But socially distant doesn't mean giving up collaboration. If we think of our classrooms as large blueprints, we can—even in a pandemic—rethink and reshape those spaces into more dynamic designs. We can still space students in ways that allow them to collaborate. We as educators can reconfigure our learning spaces to support learning in the time of COVID. We can create small footprints of gathering nooks, spaced three or six feet apart, with appropriate traffic flow patterns that allow the creative use of space and help students to learn about their classmates two desks away. We live in a time full of opportunities to engage all stakeholders around flexible seating and flexible teaching, both of which benefit our students. We must think more creatively and responsively. When the pandemic finally subsides and we return to working closely together, we'll have a perfect opportunity to blend traditional with innovative educational formats. As we discover together what lies ahead, we should continue to be prepared for change, because change will be a constant factor for the rest of our lives and our students' lives. That's why we owe it to our students to *change our own minds* about the ever-morphing shapes of learning. Students will always be faced with learning new ways to work together. And their social and emotional needs will always be vital considerations in the learning environments of any era.

In the various educational settings of my teaching career, I've learned that there will always be times when direct instruction is required. As educators, we are the ones ultimately responsible for delivering the material, methods, and support for our students. That's why I've also gathered groups in flexible formats: a corner of the room, around the couch, or at a tall table. I've taught from a chalkboard, dry erase boards, and smart screens. Students need our expertise and guidance. Some instruction is best given when students are more traditionally gathered, while other times instruction will happen informally at the side of the room or elsewhere as the need arises. The learning material will help dictate the teacher's best use of the space.

Once direct instruction is given, whether in an algebra II class, AP biology, or kindergarten handwriting practice, it's important to give students the opportunity to move about the classroom to do the work or join the teacher in small groups. This movement effectively ties traditional teaching with new and more flexible seating. It is the best of both worlds.

Educators usually don't ask for students' thoughts about classroom setup. Kids walk in, take an assigned seat, and go to work. But when we ask students what they think of the classroom furniture and design, we not only invite fresh thinking, but we tell them we trust them.

In the thirty years since our balloon project, I have moved further away from traditional furniture and teaching. I now see that *I'm* an aeronaut rising in a hot-air balloon. The miles-wide vista below me keeps expanding. Even more importantly, I'm watching student balloonists climb into the passenger baskets, ready for takeoff. We never know which ideas and projects may launch, fly, and land successfully; which ones will suddenly crash and burn; and which will float away as the results of true creativity and innovation. Naturally, though, most students and projects will need teachers to assist, encourage, extinguish small fires, and adjust their thinking to build better flying machines.

## What I Learned from Garden Beds

In my final year of teaching, my teammates and I taught ninety students to research, design, buy, and build raised garden beds for fruits and vegetables for our school. I loved watching those kids lead with such creative spark and flourishing entrepreneurship. From hot-air balloons to gardens and other projects, I climbed the learning path with my kids. We had some falls, resulting in cuts and scrapes, but we achieved what we set out to do: learn from and with each other in the best learning environments we could construct.

From simple, incremental changes in my classroom to an entire grade level working together on a yearlong project, flexible learning gave the students opportunities to thrive. Flexible seating and flexible teaching showcased learning and leading at their best.

Whether planning a garden bed layout, building tissue paper hot-air balloons, or embracing other bold ventures, I've learned that the physical space must meet the educational needs of the students and the learning tasks. Educators work with people, and people are never the same from day to day. Their learning environments should not be either.

Educators must remain flexible.

⚙ **TEACHER TIP:**
Look closely at a unit you are going to teach. Explore the opportunities to change the layout of the room to better fit the unit. Sometimes just moving a piece of furniture leads to a paradigm shift. Try it!

⚙ **TEACHER TIP:**
Give students voice to address problems they see in the classroom. Maybe their thoughts will open conversations beyond the curriculum, just as the hot-air balloons did.

# CHAPTER 3

# THE 1,000-MILE JOURNEY

I spent my entire teaching career, beginning in 1984, in public school classrooms. That included working with all types of learners: gifted and talented, special education, center-based learners, and English language learners. Most of my experience was as a general education teacher teaching language arts, science, social studies, and math to twenty-six to thirty-four students at a time.

The photo below shows my final classroom space. When students were present, every chair was occupied. Beyond the scope of the photo, other desks were clustered and occupied by students. Flexible seating allowed me to host many students in my room. Yes, it was crowded, but we still had wiggle room. I could have never crammed thirty-four desks into that space.

The layout and furniture in my final year of teaching.

As educators, we know the importance of our first day of the school year. That's when we lay a foundation for the year. We know the first impression of the room carries much weight. So, we spend hours preparing name tags, posters, folders, materials bins, lists, student supplies... the list goes on and on.

Then the students walk in on the first day of school to discover their new room. They enter not just a room, but a new psychological and emotional space where they can seek answers to their hopes and dreams as well as their dilemmas. That's also the arena where they will battle insecurities and fears. Will they know any of their classmates? What about the volume of homework? Will the teacher be friendly? Where will they sit? What if they do not have the right supplies?

What if your students went home at the end of the first *and every* day of school excited to learn because they could sit where they wanted? And what if they had a variety of seating options? What if they could tell their parents or guardians they could stand for science, sit with a friend for math, and end the day reading on one of the soft chairs, discussing a novel with the teacher?

Remember, setting up a new classroom environment takes one little change at a time. Lao Tzu was right: "The journey of a thousand miles begins with one step."

My first experience with flexible seating came in 2003-2004. At the time I did not know I had just taken the first step of a 1,000-mile journey. Because I was standing in the right place at the right time and willing to be flexible, I saw a seismic shift in education.

## Getting Outta the Box

My first classroom looked like every other room in the building: a plain square box. And that box contained my teacher's desk, individual student desks with chairs, bookshelves, and several tables. Nothing extraordinary or exciting.

Throughout my first few years of teaching, I used a large green and pink stainless-steel desk. Wherever that monster was placed in August, it stayed for the entire school year. That thing was my bunker and my warehouse. The larger the desk, the more items I could keep in it. I was known for storing copious amounts of markers, sticky notes, pens, staplers, and cute colored paper clips. When a student needed materials, I dove into my desk. I nearly always popped up, holding what they wanted.

Beside my desk, I had three bookcases: one to hold my teaching books, one for student textbooks, and one for my students' reading corner books. The room contained four bulletin boards, each on a separate wall. They were all square and mounted at the same height. I had a dry erase board on the front and back classroom walls. In those days, that whiteboard placement was the most radical step possible in blowing up cookie-cutter classroom arrangements.

My students sat in rows, facing forward, watching me as I taught. They reminded me of passengers aboard the riverboat ride at an amusement park. The passengers sat, unable to move, as the boat took them on a set course. Some passengers learned a lot because they had eagerly waited and prepared for that ride.

Others watched the clock, wishing they had a choice of other boats. I understood; they just wanted to go somewhere else (sometimes I did, too!). While they may have completed work, they showed no self-direction. That kind of classroom just wasn't a vibrant, life-giving learning space. In addition to the physical limitations, each content area existed apart from the others, and I had a specific block of time designated to teach every subject— which was necessary if we were to get through the curriculum before the spring and state testing. I was an exhausted riverboat captain, repeating the same lines over and over to bored passengers.

Even in those traditional formats, a few times each academic year I found ways to get off the riverboat with my students. I sometimes showed a movie in class. Movies were a fine alternative to traditional "sit and get" learning. Students could enjoy the movie while relaxing with friends in places of their choosing. Other off-river adventures included guest speakers. Outside voices bring a change of perspective; engaged learners would be glued to the new presenter's words, fully invested in the experience. When I changed the format, I felt like I saw my students learning to travel in their own boats, exploring the river and scenery on their own.

Movies gave fun breaks from our routine. So did allowing students to sit at the table with friends to talk about math or to read together. My students saw those changes as a gift. Was I onto something?

You and I love to choose our own places to sit in a coffee shop or bookstore. We sometimes have others we want to gather with, like family and friends. Why not allow students the same right? I increasingly noticed how confining the traditional student desks in our room were. Students could not spread out on those small surfaces. And, I realized, those kids were eagles! Or, at least, eaglets. They should have been soaring on the wind, learning the majestic heights and valleys of their environment. Instead, they seemed caged by the cramped spaces of an outmoded format.

The floor—standard industrial orange flat-pile carpet with no pad, spread over concrete—offered the only other place to sit. It became uncomfortable fast. We had no floor cushions or non-desk writing surfaces. That was prime learning space wasted.

I continued to notice that many of my kids wanted to escape their desks to sit at a table with others. They needed the social interaction, even collaboration. So, when possible and when it was conducive, I let them.

Hmm, something was going on there.

That's when I began transforming my room into a more dynamic learning space.

I had noticed that my students wanted new workspaces, opportunities to interact with others, and new furniture. *I* wanted new furniture! Why do we think office furniture went through a revolution in the last half of the twentieth century? It happened because people needed more creative and flexible shapes to accommodate their changing roles and needs. Wasn't that also true of my students? And me? And millions of other teachers? I knew I had to go big.

I decided to design a new classroom. When our school year finished on May 26, 2004, I began developing a picture of my new classroom. I wanted to invest in that vision. I was ready to tackle my dream.

**⚙ TEACHER TIP:**
Occasionally allow students to mix up their seating locations. Observe their reactions. Do they like the change? Does the change stimulate more excitement about learning? In middle and high school classes, look for opportunities to allow movement. Changing table seating, grouping tables or desks together, or adding a soft chair or two can mix up learning and increase student interactions.

## The Journey Begins

I decided to design and build my new classroom during that summer break. I wanted it ready for the fall. My principal, the only other person who knew of my vision, allotted $2,000 for my plan. Although I knew I would need more resources, I moved forward. Could my vision become reality in three months' time? *Never dream small.*

My plan was simple. I would transform my room into "Camp Colorado." Why that theme? Since our fourth grade curriculum covered Colorado history, my students would learn in an authentic Western space, complete with antiques, round tables, Western wall art, movable fixtures, and a real, life-sized wagon.

Camp Colorado, complete with Western-themed wall art and a covered wagon.

That approach to space grew out of my life. I once built a clay railroad steam engine that filled the kiln in my high school pottery class. I grasped just how big it was when I had to carry that darn thing home. It ended up as a doorstop because my parents knew how much it mattered to me. I also painted a billboard-sized hockey goalie on plywood for my high school's gymnasium. It remained there for many years after I graduated. I had always known you can use art in a big way to make a difference in people's lives. I would do the same for my fourth grade classroom.

I replaced the old student desks with five, six-foot, round pedestal tables. The tables would each easily seat six students. I planned to color coordinate everything in the room. The center of each blue laminate tabletop would hold a red, orange, yellow, blue, or green lazy Susan for community supplies.

The room would also include a large cowboy-themed bookcase to store books and supplies. With the desks being removed I would need extra storage, so I made storage covers, like saddlebags, for the backs of the students' chairs. Each one had two pouches: a small one for pencils, pens, ruler, and scissors; and a larger pouch for books and folders or spirals. The saddlebags gave my kids more workspace on the tables because they stored their supplies behind their backs, not on the work surfaces. I added mason jars for each table's common school supplies. A large sign, "Camp Colorado," was suspended in the room to invite students in. By the end of August, everything was in place

**Ask!**

Knowing my vision for the classroom would need money and community support, I had begun my quest for funds and materials as soon as school broke for the summer break in 2004. I wanted to be ready for the upcoming school year.

To make my vision happen, I learned how to *ask*. Every day I wrote letters to local citizens and companies, asking for their financial support. I worked with my city's director of small businesses to find shop owners who might help us with antiques, signage, and furnishings. I spent every workday that summer writing and printing letters on my school's letterhead stationery. And I shared the classroom layout with every business I could find. A local lumber company gave us the wood to make the tables and the wagon. A local floor covering store donated carpet to line the inside of the wagon. Over three months, I collected donations of cash and building materials to build a new learning space. My fundraising work brought in $3,200! Those donors gave more than money: They invested their hearts. People gave because they wanted to be part of something real and transformative. *I learned the only way to make it happen is to ask.*

Even when people said no, I genuinely thanked them. Most of those who declined simply couldn't support my ask right then. Sometimes "no" really means "maybe later." Fundraising is more of about a relationship than a donation. Corporations and businesses benefit from those relationships; parents, other family members, and friends love to support those business interests that sponsored the child's classroom. It becomes a win-win situation.

It was just before the school year started when we finally moved the new furniture into the classroom and assembled the tables, the wagon, and the bookshelves. Everything looked so good. And it was functional.

○ **TEACHER TIP:**
Be willing to chase your dreams when it comes to changing your classroom. If you feel the need to change things, then your students probably do too. Don't get stuck in the mud with traditional approaches. Dare to dream.

○ **TEACHER TIP:**
Consider asking your students' parents for gift cards to local furniture stores. That may provide a way to bring unique and essential pieces of furniture into the classroom. You might be surprised at their eagerness to support their child's educational environment.

## Somewhere Beyond Cool

The new patterns and forms of learning did evoke resistance from the old ones. No matter how much some people embrace change, just as many avoid or reject it. Change threatens; I know. Even fellow educators spoke to or emailed me about what I was doing, asking various iterations of, "Why should I think of changing what we have?"

I could only ask in response, "Well, how are your traditional methods and spaces working for you? Are students excited to walk into your room? *Every* day? Is your space energizing?" Sometimes I pressed deeper: "Let me ask you: Can you remember a time when teaching made your heart sing?" That question grew out of how I felt when I walked into my own transformed room.

I won some; I lost some. And I had to face it: The space I'd worked so hard to create did not meet everyone's needs. I struggled with that. But in most things, and certainly in education, we must make room for others to resist our new ideas and actions. This resistance is not personal. It reveals a way to grow. It is part of the path to learning. We won't learn if we don't try, even with physical classroom layouts.

The coolest classroom is just that: a cool-looking room, nothing more. It facilitates. But what is it that it facilitates? The soul of a classroom is the teaching philosophy *and the teacher* who animates it. And an animated teacher can make learning come alive. Students sitting in desks clumped together or in rows will sail along with the teacher's enthusiasm, even in traditional learning environments. That is the special gift of so many educators: to make magic happen in their classrooms, no matter the design of the physical space. Those are most of our educators today—dedicated people from PreK to college and beyond.

What I'm suggesting is that students might increase their learning and engagement levels even more when they can move about the room, sitting or standing, interacting with others, in groups or working individually as needed. In your own classroom, find a happy spot on this ever-expanding learning continuum. If students are uncomfortable sitting in the same spot and aren't allowed to move, they might tend to be tired and unfocused. Smoke and whistles and great bulletin boards and cool music are alluring, but they won't hide the restrictions students feel when they can't move around. I needed an inviting classroom that would support learning. In 2004 I had no blueprint or teacher's guide. I worked in a land beyond maps. In our new space my students and I had to create the blueprints and maps, and we had to do it every day. We needed something beyond the way I was using the learning space and the way I was instructing. We needed to collectively improve our learning game in the space we had.

> **○ TEACHER TIP:**
> As you think of your student outliers, think of how change in the classroom can support them. Ask them to try out a new stool or desk. Help them see that their thoughts are valued. Being trusted with a task as simple as that can provide the foundation of trust and respect those students need. Sometimes that means they will champion a particular kind or piece of furniture. That's why my folding camp chairs were a much larger hit than I had expected. I asked parents to purchase one or more chairs for the students and they willingly came through. Small asks can result in big results.

## Managing Change

Before the students even walked in the door that first day of Camp Colorado, I knew I would need routines and rhythms that would support the new arrangement. Here's why: Thirty students, each with individual needs, fears, hopes, and experiences, walk into the classroom with the potential to create harmony or chaos. Thirty eaglets, eager to fly in whatever direction they want, any time they want, can quickly create mid-air collisions. I knew it was up to me to maintain order, while respecting the hopes and dreams of my little eaglets. I did that through daily routines and rhythms. A successful year would require every eaglet to learn how to fly. The routines and rhythms would carry the peace and harmony for the room.

What does that kind of management look like in the classroom?

Five large tables and a covered wagon automatically invite people to sit, engage one another, and work together. But how could I teach the kids to learn and collaborate in the newly-designed space? How would I keep them from focusing on the cool space rather than on learning? Would the new vision succeed or flop? Would we end up back in traditional furniture? How would we build success in our learning? How would we handle assessments? State testing? What about collaborative learning? I felt like so much was riding on that space. And on me. I felt like the aeronaut watching thirty helium balloons ready to take off. Would we succeed? Would I soar or crash and burn? I was terrified.

### Who Am I?

By nature, I avoid the spotlight. So, trust me: I did not want to be the center of the change. My twin sister, my brother, and I grew up in a middle-class neighborhood in Colorado (near where I later taught). My dad was a letter carrier. Mom did not work outside our home until we were all in school.

My childhood was filled with everyday activities: bike riding, playing hide and seek, badminton, soccer, or croquet with the neighborhood kids, or watching *Batman* or *Gilligan's Island* on TV after school. In the summer we ran through the sprinklers in the backyard. In the winter we joined neighborhood snowball fights. We kids safely roamed our streets. I was not the daughter of lawyers, professors, doctors, or diplomats. I did not go to an Ivy League school. We were just a normal family down the street, and I had a normal education.

So, when what I was doing in my classroom gained attention and I became the center of a metamorphosis in learning, I guess I didn't feel like the details of my life marked me as a person of destiny. I was "Mrs. Almer," not a "change agent." Had I intruded into a place intended for someone else?

Additionally, not every student I taught loved that new learning environment. I wondered: *Was that because they needed a more charismatic leader?* Some students preferred the traditional desk and chairs. Others couldn't handle the movement and change. Some just revolted against everything. Slowly, though, I stopped personalizing it. I began to recognize their reactions as a signal that they needed help if they were going to adapt to that alternative learning environment.

One student disrupted class every day. Kenny backtalked to me, laughed at others, made inappropriate wisecracks, refused to do his work, and just generally disrupted. I came to dread taking attendance. I hoped he wouldn't show up, so we'd have a bit of peace for six hours. But Kenny came to school every day. Of course, some students were shocked that he did not like the new classroom. What wasn't to like? I learned that there are those who don't care for any learning environment. Kenny was one of these students.

His resistance and disruption challenged me that entire school year. And his obstinate behavior drew attention from others, which further drained me. True to most situations, the squeaky wheel got the most grease. And Kenny wasn't just a squeaky wheel, he was a whole set of bald tires. I hoped he wasn't headed for a cliff. But whether he did or not, I had to support the other twenty-nine students who tried to counter his disturbances.

Finally, Kenny had a breakthrough! It came through an activity in which each student had to show their expertise in something. Holly, one of the few students willing to work with him, became his partner for the activity. When she demonstrated her expertise with makeup, she chose Kenny as her client. And he sat quietly and pleasantly as she applied his makeup. As she explained the procedure with great humor, everyone laughed, including Kenny. That simple ten-minute exchange in front of his peers changed the game for him. The whole class saw him morph into a success story because of a quiet girl who helped him see who he really was. From that moment Kenny began rejoining our classroom society. We saw him work hard to curb his temper. Before the year ended, he became the kids' greatest success story. I say it was the kids' success intentionally because it wasn't as much what I did, but what the other students did—the love and respect the students showed him in our fluid space—that made the difference to and for him. That too is what flexible seating can do. It helped a troubled kid, an outcast, become part of the community.

In another school year, a student named Jane was critical of the classroom design. She didn't like the community vibes in the room. Schoolwork was difficult for her. She blocked everything we wanted to do in class. Unfortunately, Jane's story did not turn out well. I hated that she was one who slipped through the cracks, a few years later dropping out of school as a teenager. I did my best, but I was never sure how to reach some students. I learned if I was going to understand and help the Kennys and Janes of my world, I had to learn where they were coming from. I had to know their stories. In time, I saw that they were just angry, no matter what I or anyone else said or did. I (and some students) gave them space and gave them grace. I tried to support them, but when they wouldn't allow me to help them, I had to just keep them from threatening the learning or safety in the classroom.

I also discovered that, for some of my students like Kenny and Jane, I might be the only person who would give them a side hug, a smile, or a high five. My role was not only that of a teacher but also that of a friend, a champion, a cheerleader. I discovered that I must greet every student when they walked into my room with eye contact, a smile, and a "Good morning!" to set the tone for the day. I saw Jane and Kenny and others like them as people more than students. Even if I only saw a student for a forty-five-minute marine biology class, I could still affirm him or her as an individual. The impact of kindness can last a very long time.

○ **TEACHER TIP:**
It is okay if a student needs to sit in a particular chair and nowhere else in the room. Learn to flex with your students and you'll discover that they will give more in return. Some benefit from a traditional chair or desk. See each of them for who they are as a person and a learner and let them have that space as well. Don't throw out everything you have in your room for new and innovative furniture. Change can be slow, simple, and minor. But sometimes small changes are all you need to create a successful learning space.

○ **TEACHER TIP:**
Remember the breakthroughs and successes. Too often educators focus on the one bad story in the class, not the thirty-two success stories. Keep an electronic file of positive emails, notes, parent support, and student comments. Celebrate breakthroughs and successes as they come.

# CHAPTER 4

# WHAT IS FLEXIBLE SEATING?

The educational foundation Edutopia, founded by filmmaker George Lucas, has been one of the major drivers of K-12 flexible seating. In a 2015 article, Edutopia made the case for flexibility well and succinctly: "Flexible classrooms give students a choice in what kind of learning space works best for them, and helps them to work collaboratively, communicate, and engage in critical thinking."[1]

I agree. I've seen students in flexible classrooms become more invested and successful in their learning. Student voice and choice make an enormous difference. A vibrant classroom filled with thriving students is one of the most beautiful things I've ever seen. Students don't want to leave at the end of the day. Often, teachers don't either! Flexible classrooms can take many forms—they don't all have to be Camp Colorado. A flexible classroom can be the simple addition of three optional seats or the use of a short table instead of all tall tables; twenty-five desks with three seating options and an ottoman; ten drafting tables and a couch; or thirty individual desks with chairs and a sofa. Flexible classrooms allow students times to gather and sit/work in various spots they may not be assigned to, or it lets them sit with people they might not normally sit near, either during the day, the class period, the week, the semester, the social studies unit, the chemistry experiment, or the soap box derby car assembly. Being flexible can look like moving a few tables or desks for the morning or afternoon, or for just a class period or two. Or, based on need, it could look like completely transforming the learning space.

My K-12 education took place in traditional classrooms with rows of evenly-spaced seats and desks, all facing forward. Every day, I would walk into my classroom and find my seat in the middle of row three. Sometimes, *if I were lucky*, I could choose to sit by a friend *as long as* we did our work and remained quiet. That was flexible seating in its infancy. Thankfully, that idea flowered into the dynamic learning environments we see today.

Creating a physical and flexible learning environment has hit the educational world like a tsunami over the past few years. Yes, it rearranged some traditional coastlines. But more and more researchers, educators, school districts, and educational vendors have seen the transformative benefit of the fresh forms on the learning environment. A flexible environment allows educators to fluidly and successfully move within traditional and hybrid models.

Flexible learning allows students to lean into their work. Furniture is a big deal in most living, work, and institutional spaces. So of course furniture carries enormous influence within the educational space. Furniture must be flexible so it can be quickly and easily reconfigured to meet diverse educational tasks. The teacher is no longer the "Sage on the Stage," the sole possessor and imparter of knowledge in the room, and flexible learning environments reflect that reality.

When I kept the same configuration, we called it "Homebase." That was a predetermined setup with specific assigned seats. I made students responsible for the movement and care of the furniture. That saved time and avoided chaos when we needed to change things. Everyone had a job and did it quickly.

To help guest teachers when I could not be there, I created a three-ring notebook or an online file folder complete with guest teacher lesson plans, general classroom management sheets, diagrams and photos of the room arrangements for each subject, supplies maintenance, student class lists, and anything else that would make the day run smoothly. I let my teammates know where the notebook or online folder was located.

When I was in later elementary school, I had one teacher who was a paragon of old-school teaching. Every day she'd stand at the front of the classroom and write on the old blackboard with powdery white chalk. In perfect cursive, she would write long outlines of everything we had to learn in that class. As students, our job was to copy what she wrote on the board, precisely as she did, onto our lined sheets of college-ruled notebook paper, in blue or black ink (we were also graded on the notebook's neatness). We wrote her outlines word for word and then memorized them word for word.

My teacher would fill the whole chalkboard wall with notes, then walk to the back of the room and continue talking as she wrote on the second blackboard. When she finished there, she'd move back to the front of the room where she would erase the initial notes and continue writing. That would go on for forty-five minutes! Pity the poor soul who didn't get them copied in time! This teacher was the expert. We just listened and wrote. We didn't need to look up anything, think anything, or ask anything. Her students learned nothing more than how to copy neatly onto paper, in blue or black ink, and in cursive. I can't remember much of anything from those notes. I had no investment in the learning; I was not an active participant in my knowledge base.

Thankfully, educator roles have transformed into that of facilitator *and learner* right along with, and sometimes as much as, the students. We all seek knowledge. Facilitators guide the learning process, ask questions, give suggestions, and offer insights. But the crux of the learning rests in the students' hands, as it did with my fourth graders and their hot-air balloons.

As a teacher, my classrooms morphed through four different stages as my students and I discovered what we needed to sustain and strengthen our learning paths. Through every success and setback, I learned to not only transform a space, but to make the mind shift necessary to make it all work. In the beauty of freedom and fluidity, the students and I filled the roles of both sages and facilitators. We all learned we were responsible, individually and collectively, for our facility and our processes. And we all had agency!

Flexible seating allowed both the students and me to move according to the need of the moment. Students could move to different places as it was helpful. They were in charge of those choices; I tried to always permit and encourage those little eaglets to spread their wings as they saw the potential of who they could be. What a joy to see them soar with the wind. Did every student love that environment? No. Some preferred the traditional furniture. If "flexibility" means anything, it must mean all students should be able to work in the furniture that supports their own preferences. Yes, even if that means that some may want to return to more conventional furniture. Everyone needs to work where they can attain their best. I included conventional furniture—traditional desks, tables, and chairs—as other learning spots. Just as airlines may allow passengers to make changes in the row, aisle, or seat for more comfort, I did, too. Small things can make a world of difference. Success arrives through various seating options.

○ **TEACHER TIP:**
   Allow your students to make little changes in their seating. Even changing the direction their chair faces can make a more positive and friendlier learner.

## So, What Does Flexible Space Look Like?

My teaching spaces always buzzed with movement; lots of hustle and bustle in the room! Kids putting materials away, getting supplies, finding a place to sit, chatting with their friends. There was typically a relaxed, friendly hum in the room. The kids (and I) were happy to be filling our space and working with each other. I loved how that tone set our days for success. We were a community of learners. More important than that, we began our days as people with hopes, hurts, needs, and stories to share from what happened the night before or on the way to school. We looked forward to the day. Mesquite, Texas ISD Superintendent David Vroonland calls that buzz a "collective hum." It's the sound of a coffee shop, of collaboration, and of contentment.

Each morning, students entered the room talking. We raised the blinds to pull the morning into the room. A flurry of activity marked the awakening of the room. Students chose space within the small clusters of nooks. Soon, every spot was taken. We opened and filled our space with purpose and intentionality. When we all came together, we'd sit on the floor or stand in a circle. The activity and settling into certain rhythms set the tone for our work and strengthened our bonds as a community.

Middle school and high school classrooms can reflect this same atmosphere. Flexibility is not only about the space, but about the conversations shared. Spending the first five minutes to inquire about everyone's day or evening keeps students grounded together. I've seen teachers in middle school place a mailbox in their room near the classroom door where students could place notes for the teacher to read after class, asking for support. These are safe ways for students to be seen and heard.

During any emergency or crisis, including coping with the COVID pandemic, it's important to continue living and working in community, to continue allowing students space to share and be seen. Our connectedness pulls the community into a common thread of support and cohesion, one that lets all the members know they have full permission to be noticed and heard. That's because they matter—to the community and within any crisis. I always allowed, even encouraged, students to share personal things—human touches—during those times we celebrated or lamented as a group.

Because we had built this environment of sharing and support, through difficult times my students and I carried each other in our collective hands and hearts. I cried with my students the morning I learned my father-in-law had died. As I left to be with my family, the students circled around me and gave me a big class hug. I remember some crying as I left the classroom. Another time, I told my class I was pregnant with my first child. They wanted to give me a baby shower then and there! I remember when Zelda, a student from Yugoslavia, announced she had to return to that country, but she didn't want to leave us. We were all an emotional mess that morning.

Morning meetings were the Elmer's glue in my classrooms. They held and sustained us through each day. Many times, we also convened a closing meeting before leaving at the day's end. We needed to share what we had seen, heard, touched, and felt during that day.

With each subject, we shifted the furniture to meet the learning task. My ability to reach any part of the room quickly was known as "breaking the four corners of the room." No longer could the back of the room become the place where students could goof off. Besides the greater freedom and creativity, the flexible space also maintained order. It allowed no place for mischief to hide.

Even in a pandemic, flexible learning space can still accommodate collaboration and vibrant learning. Clearly marked traffic flow paths help promote student safety. And the strategic placement of sanitary wipe stations helps to disinfect furniture, books, writing instruments, and other surfaces. Movement is healthy; bodies need exercise, fresher air, and relief from being pinned in one spot. We can collaborate. We just need to build more space and movement into the formula.

In middle school and high school, furniture doesn't always have to shift every period to meet every need. A simple shift of tables or chairs each week can add an extra element to excite students as they choose where they'd like to sit or stand. With older students, focusing on chair rearrangements is easy and quick to manage. Or, move tables or desks to the back of the room and sit more casually on the floor for a day or two. Move desks or tables toward the center of the room, placing chairs on the outer perimeter. Place desks into triads in the center and corners of the room, with tables around them as dividers or nook definers. Suspend chart paper from the ceiling near each nook. Let students move throughout each and they'll figure out where they learn best.

⚙ **TEACHER TIP:**
Prioritize squeezing in time each day for team or class meetings. Something as simple as a ten minute, "How are we doing today?" Letting everyone have a moment to speak creates a classroom community students become bound into. Students in upper-level classes need that connection, too. Moving from class to class with different teachers and peers can make one feel alone or invisible. Connecting like this lets students know they are seen and heard, not just one of thirty-five kids in AP English or World Literature, seventh grade PE, or the entire third grade.

In summary, flexible seating is not a magic bullet. It's an *attitude*. More than furniture, it's a *philosophy*, one that transcends how we sit and work to impact the ways we talk and interact with one another. According to author and futurist Rex Miller,

> Changing space shines a spotlight on culture. All the
> drama of a company comes to life when you meddle
> with the way people live. All the subterranean politics
> and conflicts surface; they come to life. When you
> change space... there is not one element of the company
> that doesn't have a stake and doesn't show up.[2]

Rex identified the thrill and the threat of changing space. And
that is true anytime, anywhere. When you "meddle with the
way people live," they respond quickly and firmly. Inanimate
objects are not the issue. Those are just proxies for their lives,
and their lives are what you're actually touching. You can release
or constrain how they work, create, flourish. So be respectful.
Recognize that the people in your environment are stakeholders
in the future. Treat them like it.

**⚙ TEACHER TIP:**
Morning Meetings or quick gatherings at the start of
a class period are great ways to gather kids together
to build community and cohesion in the classroom. All
ages in K-12 need to be heard, seen, and understood as
individuals. These meetings can start small with getting
to know each other's food, pet, hobby, sports, music, and
movie preferences. The more we learn about each other,
the more we can know and support each other.

**⚙ TEACHER TIP:**
Remember that the furnishings in the classroom are
important to everyone. So, talk to your students about
their preferences for seating and for learning. When you
do, you may find that giving them a voice is even more
important than the furniture.

# CHAPTER 5

# THE PLAN UNFOLDS

On that first day of the Camp Colorado classroom, my students walked into the new environment in a full chorus of "Ooh," "Wow," and "Awesome." When they asked me for their seat assignments, I told them what I had wanted to say for a long time: "Please sit anywhere you want." As they ran to choose favorite spots and save seats for their friends, the room quickly filled up.

Each table group got to set the rules and purpose for how to use their lazy Susans, the eight cubbies in their table containing common items for community sharing, and other communal storage. Each table took different paths to make those decisions. I let them work through that alone. I didn't assign group managers or timekeepers. The discussions flowed freely as I made notes about leaders, listeners, den mothers, and other group dynamics. That information would come in handy later.

Giving students voice and choice allowed them to see that they had ownership in our room. That was vital to the "collective hum." Because the furniture was so new, they had more reason to care for their learning space. On that first day of school, I had introduced team building without them realizing it.

Jane was the obstinate voice in the room. She didn't buy into any of the furniture and didn't want any part of sharing. We still had two single student desks and chairs in the room; she claimed one of them as her territory. Her eyes defied anyone to contradict her. She remained defiant all year. But her voice still mattered; we hoped she would come around and even contribute to the positive culture of learning. We'd have to wait and see.

Once we had the storage space figured out at each table, we worked through other management and flow issues in our room, like movement, independent or group work, and use of the wagon.

Teams discussed each item, then shared their group thinking with the class. I documented the contributions and questions. The class voted on each issue. Everyone could see that every voice mattered and was heard. We discussed the free exchange of ideas, the principle of majority rule, and how to live with the decisions reached through the voting. I suggested an anchor chart for a Class Constitution, documenting the decisions made by everyone in the room. We agreed to keep the rules short (ten or fewer), and to the point. We would not get bogged down in minutia. All students signed the document, and we posted it in the room. I permitted classes to amend the Constitution from time to time as needed.

I knew that some educators felt that a democratic approach gave students too much freedom and power. And some feared that freedom and power might cause the educators to lose control of the classroom. I didn't allow that to happen. A line at the bottom of the chart plainly stated the teacher had the right to move students when they were not being their best selves. They couldn't argue with that.

Even in FLEX-ED, learning comes first.

Students sitting together at an open table did not compromise privacy or test integrity. I kept a set of trifold privacy screens and noise-cancelling headphones available for anyone. Students who needed private space simply placed a screen around their spot on the table, used the headphones, or both. These techniques can translate to most teaching environments.

○ **TEACHER TIP:**
If you are not ready to implement free seating/learning all day, try it for one subject a week. Start small.

○ **TEACHER TIP:**
Remember, although the changes in your room will be exciting to most, it is okay if not everyone loves the changes. Keeping a foot in the traditional while moving into the new is acceptable. It provides the grounding some students need to feel comfortable with changes.

○ **TEACHER TIP:**
It is often better for a teacher to listen more than he or she talks. Speaking less can be more effective when trying to understand students.

## Our Anchor Space

We can all agree with Dorothy in *The Wizard of Oz*: "There's no place like home." Everyone needs that safe space of freedom, protection, and support. I found that also applied to classrooms. Students need a dedicated space to gather. *Home.*

That's the real reason I designed and built the covered wagon. I wanted a bigger, better, safer place where my students could relax and be themselves. That covered wagon became an anchor for us, our home. The students decided when and how we would use it. That alone gave them more voice and choice in the nature and purpose of the room. One rule: They had to leave their shoes outside the wagon when they entered.

Although my wagon could hold fifteen fifth graders, the class voted to limit the number to eight. They also decided each table group could use it as their workspace one day of each week. The students could also decide if they wanted the white twinkle lights illuminated or off when it was their turn in the wagon.

Giving them ownership provided a greater sense of care and agency for the students. They knew it was *their* space.

If you were a third, fourth, or fifth grader, wouldn't you be more engaged if you could learn in a covered wagon? Creative learning spaces help young imaginations soar. One of my daughter's classrooms had an oversized bathtub (without water, of course) as an anchor space. She and her classmates could sit inside the tub to read. What a fun way to leave the world behind and dive into a good book!

When I started this journey into flexible classrooms, I did not know the great potential and transformations it would allow. My students and I were like pioneers exploring the Wild West together. My anchor spaces evolved over time; they haven't always been covered wagons. I've also had couches, a bench, and a pair of chairs. They all served the purpose of creating a collective gathering space. None of the others were as fancy or as large as the wagon, yet all the spaces brought us together. An anchor space can be as simple as a comfortable couch and chair with an oval rug. It can also be as innovative as the loft treehouse one teacher built for her room.

○ **TEACHER TIP:**
Every classroom space needs an anchor. Something as simple as tape marked on the floor can create a common area. It doesn't have to be elaborate; it just needs to serve the purpose of bringing people together. It can be as simple as a table marked with colored tape as a gathering space for students in middle school or high school. This kind of slight change can make a big difference as it acknowledges the importance of gathering in a place where everyone can be seen and heard. And that's the real point: It's not about furniture. The classroom tells every student, "Your voice matters in this place!"

## Movement

Naturally, I sometimes had to impose different seating arrangements for certain times or tasks. Occasionally imposing seating arrangements was also helpful for other reasons. It gave the opportunity to have students leave their hamster wheels. It also taught them to live flexibly within their social arrangements and work patterns. I could also see that change brought a sense of newness to the room. Seeing the classroom from a different location provided a helpful psychological shift.

At the beginning of the year of Camp Colorado, I told everyone their cubbies, chairs, and saddlebags were theirs for the year. As expected, Jane kept to her individual desk and chair. She, like everyone, needed to feel grounded. For her, that meant sticking to the traditional furniture. That arrangement supported her sense of identity (just as the new shapes supported others). A room like this had never existed in that school. Whether a student liked or rejected the space as a whole, I knew everyone needed a comfortable and safe spot to call their own.

Changes in work and living space sometimes call for *more* rules, at least until new patterns of movement, speech, collaboration, and time management become ingrained. We openly discussed and voted on procedures for bathroom, drinks, getting supplies, and physical transitions in the room. We kept the rules simple and few. And we practiced drills and procedures until we all knew what was expected. Because everything was so new, I could see that establishing routines at the start of the year would prevent chaos later. The room remained a work in progress as we ironed out the kinks.

Although the transformation was an organic one and the kids adapted quickly, I often felt the need for control. With all the change swirling around me, I was tempted to orchestrate every moment. As soon as I learned to relax and trust the kids, I realized they were okay with the new arrangements. They adapted quickly. Maybe I could, too! I found a new sense of freedom in my teaching and within our new environment of learning. I expected the best from my students. And from myself.

We all came through!

That year turned out to be an important turning point for me. Seeing my students take ownership and pride in the classroom, moving furniture, solving problems, and engaging the tools and terms of their learning felt better than I could have imagined. The classroom was vibrant and life-giving for all of us.

○ **TEACHER TIP:**
Human beings aren't meant to stay stationery. Foot tapping, rocking gently back and forth, and wiggling can help anyone when they need to think. This is natural and should be allowed.

○ **TEACHER TIP:**
Some classrooms must have established, specific routines for safety purposes. Middle and high school family and consumer science classes, tech ed, drama classes occurring on stage, science rooms with lab equipment— all need boundaries to be successful. Whatever the room and learning circumstance, routines and rhythms for success should always be established as priorities.

## Parent and Teacher Reactions to the Flexible Classroom

In the face of such change, my students' parents handled the new classroom very well. At Back to School Night, my students walked into our classroom with their families. Most parents looked around in amazement. From their comments, I could tell most saw the space as an inviting and relaxing place to learn. Some asked why that approach wasn't being used in other rooms. Some spoke of their child's love for our new learning space. Parents seeing their child that happy is what fully endorsed the change.

Jane's parents were a different story. Jane had told them she hated the classroom. But when they saw the space, they were completely and pleasantly surprised. From Jane's descriptions they came expecting something out of a horror movie. I explained the philosophy behind the room's design and the focus on students' comfort and learning. They wanted to see where she sat. When I pointed them to her desk, it didn't surprise them. They hoped she would join the class in seeing the space's positives. I promised to keep them apprised of her progress.

Collectively, those of us on the school campus did have to navigate the impact of our new classroom on the rest of the school. Most kids adapted fine to the other classrooms. But a teacher told me one of my students couldn't adapt to that teacher's classroom. The teacher felt the flexible seating in my room was the reason. That kind of reaction seemed like a normal response to change, and we worked through it. The student learned to work within several different learning environments and became better for it. All of life, including education and the working world, presents many environments in which to live and work. The cookie-cutter approach broke down a long time ago. Diversity and flexibility now bring out the best in those who occupy these assorted environments. Encountering a variety of classroom settings allows learners to grow and thrive.

Through all of this, I recognized that we all had much to learn as a community caught in a rapidly-changing world. School furniture would probably be just a catalyst to expose individual attitudes toward that journey.

**⚙ TEACHER TIP:**
Change can thrill and it can threaten, both at the same time. Expect any change to provoke different responses in different people. These reactions aren't personal attacks against you. Rather, they are normal human responses; people need some degree of control of their own environments, and you are asking them to rethink

what that looks like. Flex with them when you can and continue to move forward with your classroom vision.

# CHAPTER 6

# THE NEXT MOVE FORWARD

To build on the success of Camp Colorado, I decided to add a new type of seating in my room: swivel tractor stools! Why? Because I love tractor stools. My enthusiasm for them carried over to the kids. Long ago, I learned to share my enthusiasm. We are all "carriers" of our own excitement and beliefs. Let others catch them. Other people, especially school kids, will often match your zest for life. Jane wasn't on board with the tractor stools; I hoped she would get there. But we rolled on.

I placed the stools around the kidney-shaped reading corner table as alternatives to the regular desk chairs. When the students saw them, I felt I was watching the grand opening of a new ride at an amusement park. Kids pulled stools from under the table, dropped their backpacks to the floor, and started pushing each other around the room. We heard laughter and screams as stools bumped into other furniture and students all around the room. I quickly learned that anything on wheels, like those tractor stools, will become something for kids to ride. After the stools were placed back under the table, I reminded them that the

My students and I loved the addition of tractor stools.

stools' purpose was to provide a place to sit while at the table, not to use for racing around the classroom. What a thrilling way to start our morning!

Those tractor seats brought so much energy to our room, further increasing the vibrancy of our learning space. We had tractor stools, student chairs, the wagon, and the floor for sitting. We were evolving together in our discovery of fresh forms that gave more options and flexibility to learn.

> ⚙ **TEACHER TIP:**
> When a change in the classroom isn't accepted as you hope, don't take it personally. Some classes don't mix well with unconventional furniture. Just store the piece in a closet until later in the month or year, when you can try it again. Students may just need time to adjust to the options.

At the end of that year, I asked my students what they had liked most. I expected comments about the lunch bunches I held throughout the year, or the cool science experiments. But Reggie said, "This classroom is more flexible than other classes, which aren't modern. They just have a few desks or different chairs. I don't learn as well in those."

Sonia answered, "When you're comfortable or relaxed, your brain isn't focused on anything else, just learning."

Then Ashley spoke. "I want all classes to be this way because I can be more wrapped up in my learning." The wisdom they so honestly yet passionately shared was genuine and spot-on. I was moved to hear ten- and eleven-year-old kids express their passion and thanks for giving them the opportunity and the tools to help them find themselves. The furniture was a gift that allowed them to create and discover curiosity. They were learning how to adapt to various physical learning spaces in their school. I saw that make them better learners, but more importantly, it also helped them to better cope with challenges in their lives. Our classroom proved to be supportive in ways other classrooms were not. It was as simple as that.

The "4 C's" of twenty-first century skills—critical thinking, collaboration, communication, and creativity[3]—are necessary for those who want to participate in the global economy. So, clearly, they must also be practiced in classrooms. Learning spaces provide the perfect opportunity for students to think flexibly in the face of challenges. Students practice the "4 C's" as they address social, emotional, academic, and intellectual needs. There are many examples of how we can help make this happen:

- Giving students the freedom to choose who they work with, whenever possible and appropriate (the social-emotional need)

- Helping students understand the "voice volume" issue and ramifications (the academic and environmental need)

- Helping students learn their voices are valued and heard (the social-emotional need)

- Affirming students when they exhibit creative ways to show their understanding of any academic topic, like the three viewpoints held by the Colonists during the Revolutionary War (the intellectual need)

- Helping students understand appropriate and inappropriate life lessons and choices (social, emotional, and intellectual needs)

- Helping students' voices decipher their responses to me and my instruction, whether as a leader or learner in our room (academic need)

Finally, the "4 C's" demonstrate that student and teacher voices must be of equal weight and equally honored in the classroom.

Students and teachers spend an average of seven hours a day, five days a week, in the classroom. That's over 1,300 hours in a normal school year. Clearly, if we expect students and teachers to thrive, we should make school spaces as inviting as possible. With that goal in mind, I learned to ask foundational questions about the learning environment before the start of any school year. It all comes down to classroom management and activity. Let us look at these factors more closely.

○ **TEACHER TIP:**
Asking your students for their reactions and advice can be a golden nugget, maybe one of the best you'll ever discover as a teacher. Student honesty will help you carry classroom changes further than anyone could imagine. After all, students are vital stakeholders, essential clients of your work. They matter. Listen to them.

### General Classroom Management

With a dynamic learning environment, I needed to figure out how to manage my classroom. Flexible does not mean a loss of structure—everyone doing what they want, when they want, and wherever they want. People need rhythms and routines to function. But the details of (and strategies for) a more dynamic environment will always change according to personality and situation. Some educators work well in a loosely structured room; others prefer tighter forms and greater control.

My teaching style fell in the middle of those two poles. I did not allow interference with the learning environment, no matter who was doing the teaching or the learning. Not going to happen with me. But I also liked for students to share the instructional role. Instructing encourages deeper learning and leadership development. The memory and mastery of a task increase when we can teach what we know to others. Magic comes when that happens organically in a given environment.

At its most basic, the command and transfer of knowledge are the aims of education. To fulfill that on my watch, I preferred to approach students and situations with an open heart and patience. I often said to students, "Because I care about and respect you and every other student in here, this behavior cannot continue. Your behavior distracts learning in this place. We can chat about this in a few minutes when I am free to give you my full attention. In the meantime, please work on your own. Thank you." In that way, I tried to honor those students by letting them know I saw, heard, and valued them, even when their actions weren't appropriate.

○ **TEACHER TIP:**
Too many teachers think of classroom management and classroom discipline as synonyms. They are not. Management means effective teacher support of the learning environment. Discipline is a corrective and essential reaction to inappropriate behavior. Working together to achieve cohesiveness for everyone in the learning environment is key. This helps to create a manageable and positive classroom environment.

## Activity

Because classrooms contain people, they will always be very dynamic arenas. People move. As a teacher, my general rule was to permit student movement, if it didn't interfere with learning. If you walked into any of my classrooms, you would probably not have seen students sitting the entire class period. Movement and activity were constant and natural parts of my classrooms.

My rooms were like pinball machines: bells and whistles, flashing lights, plungers, ramps, paths, and flippers, all working together to support the pinball as it accumulated points. Just as freedom to move helps in playing pinball, it also allows for easier and more spontaneous teamwork among students. I saw the many parts of our "pinball classroom" come together every day to create an open and active learning space everyone loved.

At the end of each day, my students were appropriately exhausted from their intense and physically active learning. I celebrated that; it meant they had taken over the workload, and I was there to support. I saw this as evidence of autonomous learning at its best. I always found purposeful activity to be a good thing. I experienced much less stress when I let activity percolate in the room. Students learned they didn't need permission to move around. Active and happy students were eager to work with others and complete assignments. They created fewer problems, too.

I always found *trust given was trust earned*, and granting freedom of movement communicated trust. In that way activity became a measure of trust, and building and sharing trust is crucial to an open classroom environment. I know that students sitting in assigned seats for an entire class period become antsy and unfocused. They need to break out, move, walk around, and talk with others. In some moments, so many heads nodded from drowsiness, I thought I had a class of bobbleheads. Caffeine (for me!) or movement (for all of us) were our only options to wake up! The class was sometimes like a rocket on the launch pad, seconds before takeoff. Occasionally I'd have to pause the countdown, which caused pressure to build. Activity relieves tension and boredom, and it helps the brain to reengage. When brains are engaged it creates a classroom culture of intentional investigation. The feel and buzz of that kind of room is like a coffee shop, where everyone enjoys sitting in their favorite spot, talking to friends, and is free to move as needed. I wished my room could have a latte machine to complete the ambience. I did provide surprise hot chocolate on wintry mornings, especially when snow was falling. Marshmallows were optional!

I wanted my students to be as happy and playful as puppies. When puppies sniff and tumble their way around a yard, they capture the sheer joy of exploration. It should work the same for humans; curiosity should be fun, not punishing. I know there will always be times when students talk about something unrelated to education. That is human nature. No big deal; a simple nod from me was usually all it took to nudge them back on task. We had developed mutual trust.

Activity is important to keep the brain active. I found it to be ideal if students could move out of their seats every twenty minute to stimulate the brain's neurons. When I first heard of this, I thought, "Every twenty minutes? I'm not through a lesson in twenty minutes!" But then I realized I didn't sit still when I taught, and my students didn't need to sit still for an entire class period to learn. Movement would help to keep them awake. I implemented activities as simple as tossing a beanbag around to stimulate physical movement. It worked. One afternoon when my class couldn't work through a math problem, I brought out the beanbags. We spent seven or eight minutes throwing them around. As soon as we finished, they were able to solve the problem. I always kept beanbags ready. Sometimes students played catch with them, or one student might play with one while working out a problem. Who would have thought that small bags of beans could bring a fresh viewpoint or help kids solve problems?

○ **TEACHER TIP:**
   How do you show your students you trust them? Find ways to allow freedom—like sitting somewhere different. Try it. Break some molds and traditions. Even small allowances during a class period to shift and move make a big difference.

○ **TEACHER TIP:**
   Provide students with other simple handheld tools or devices to help them work through stress or difficult work in the classroom. Items like stress balls or hourglass timers give students opportunities to de-stress.

○ **TEACHER TIP:**
   Allow older students to take notes inside coloring books.

Writing inside the lines of a drawing gives the brain stimulation while cementing a visual picture with notes and icons. Coloring the pictures is calming, too. I've heard of high school teachers allowing this as a way to keep notes. It works.

## Seating Options and Learning Preferences

Students who have specific needs make learning preferences important in the classroom. Students with hearing or visual impairments require special considerations so that they can learn along with everyone else.

Before the first day of each school year, my front office or the school nurse informed me of any special needs and how best to address them. That too was part of developing a dynamic and flexible learning classroom. Physical impairments were like any other accommodation: Just make it easy and inconspicuous. No need to call attention to it; provide the tools and atmosphere necessary for everyone to learn best.

Seating is a primary educational issue, for the same reason it is a major factor in offices, theaters, courtrooms, libraries, and other spaces. Seating supports and releases people to pursue the purpose that brings them to the room. Students come to class to learn. Seating should provide solid support for that purpose.

When I introduced the seating options to my classrooms, I explained the details for how to use the furniture. I even placed plastic frames in each area. Each frame held a photo of the area or a clever name and the number of students who could be accommodated there.

For example, the following photo shows two different seating area signs. The *I Survived Series* sign includes four small rectangles, meaning four students could sit in that area. The *Charlotte's Web* sign shows space for two kids. One class also

Framed signs designate different seating areas. The rectangles indicate how many students can use each area at a time.

used four camping chairs around a small coffee table. With one on each side, four students could work together around the coffee table.

In another class, I let three students sit on the couch, using a coffee table for their things. In upper-level classrooms, the opportunity to switch a table or desk position during a period provides a welcome change and breath of fresh air.

To help my students learn the different types of seating and which worked best for them, I gave everyone a clothespin with their name on it. Each day every student picked a place to sit and placed their clothespin on the sign in that spot. Rotating students through every type of seating took several weeks, depending on the amount of time we allowed for each. By the end of that trial period, students had figured out which seating they preferred. Middle and high school classrooms won't need as much time to make seating decisions and those students will probably have great additional thoughts about room arrangements.

I use seating or standing preference information when I need to intentionally group students. This valuable information lends itself to supporting students' specific needs and it creates a more engaging classroom for purposeful learning situations.

I don't remember any courses in classroom furniture in my education or teaching certification process. Maybe there should have been. Furniture options are diverse in their design, construction, and technologies and can accommodate so many human differences. It also seems every decade rewrites the procedures and possibilities when it comes to classroom furniture. Teachers must know that continually expanding topic just as much as they know all the subject areas.

**○ TEACHER TIP:**
Seating options are just that: options. Flex when students suddenly decide the chair, stool, or pillow doesn't work. Let them shift. Making a big deal out of the little things will drive you and the students crazy; they will feel you aren't honoring their learning needs, and they will be less willing to work. No one likes being strapped down in one seat all day.

**○ TEACHER TIP:**
Middle and high school classrooms can be as flexible as elementary rooms. Allowing seating or standing options gives everyone the opportunity to discover the ways they learn best. The room doesn't have to be completely transformed, especially when each forty-five- to sixty-minute period means teaching a different grade level or subject. Grouping tables or desks for a period and then having students pull tables together for the next class provides enough change for everyone to see the potential in the physical layout, and it invites more voice and choice in the learning. If this seems too much, consider moving the furniture for a week's unit of study, then switching into a different configuration the next.

## CHAPTER 7

# CREATING GROUNDING SPACES

We often think of the idiom "as the crow flies" as referring to the fastest way to get from one point to another.

But that is not always the best route in education. We work with humans. Taking the fastest way can sometimes injure, discourage, or impede them. We often must slow down. As we looked at earlier, the railroad crossing warning applies to many people, certainly teachers:

**STOP—LOOK—LISTEN.**

Pay attention to that young person standing in front of you. What does she or he need—from you, from the room, from the lesson, from life? Is she hungry? Is he frightened? Could confusion, grief, pain, poverty, or disability be factors here? As one sign behind an auto parts service counter reminded employees,

**THE PERSON STANDING IN FRONT OF YOU IS NOT AN INTERRUPTION OF YOUR WORK. HE OR SHE IS THE PURPOSE OF IT.**

That wisdom applies to every classroom.

Sometimes when the chosen path is closed because of rocks or other debris in the road, we must take detours. And that means slow down: stop, look, and listen. We may need more time before we can return to the main road. As a teacher, I learned it was rare when my teaching days unfurled as planned. I so often thought of Ralph Waldo Emerson's line, "To finish the moment, to find the journey's end in every step of the road, to live the greatest number of good hours, is wisdom." I also believe his insight, "It's not the destination, it's the journey."

"Grounding" can mean many things, depending on the specific disciplines or practitioners using the term. But to me, as a teacher, it meant being connected, content, and confident in my place and my role, supporting students as they discovered their place in the learning process. Through grounding, I learned to focus on the *why* around my teaching before the how, when, who, or what. Looking at, listening to, and learning from the students standing right in front of me gave me the WHY for my classroom transformations. It was for them!

*How* I transformed my classrooms was more complex. But a strong *why* kept illuminating my path as I walked. And that gave me the courage to keep trying, seeking, and reinventing. It also gave me the boldness to ask for support from community, corporate, and individual donors.

### The Practical Benefits of Stop—Look—Listen

Because I had no handbook, website, FAQs, or counsel for what I did, I had to practice Stop—Look—Listen every day. Some of what I learned may help you to remain grounded. So, let's look at some practical points of that approach:

1. **Learn to embrace detours.** They can uncover hidden treasures you wouldn't find along the main road.

2. **Build your space.** I love treehouses. As a child, we never had one because our backyard tree was too small. But my sister and I built a cozy nook in our closet, covering the doorway with pink curtains and filling the space with pillows. That

became our getaway spot. Most teachers and students need something similar. Make your getaway spot as creative as you wish. The sky's the limit; everyone deserves and needs a special getaway for more creative work and free-form learning.

3. **Create and furnish a classroom anchor**. The classroom anchor provides a focal point, a gathering place. It's somewhat like the keel in a sailing vessel; it keeps the craft upright in all seas. As you've already seen, one of my classes used a wagon. Other items—a couch, a bench, a pair of chairs, a rocking chair, even a plastic rowboat—can serve the same purpose. Unusual, inviting visual pieces draw students together into "stop, look, and listen" community moments.

Here are two of the other grounding anchor pieces I've used in my classrooms:

4. **Design other spaces.** Teachers can always inject color and zest into the classroom's boring or exhausted spots. I advise any teachers to study their classroom. Consider changing one corner of the room. What about the classroom library or reading corner? Could that be the place to start? A science or literacy organizational area? My husband built a three-foot-tall, three-panel divider to separate an area like this from the rest of the room. I added pillows and books, completing the corner as a tranquil place to read. Just a little creative thinking made that space possible.

○ **TEACHER TIP:**
Stop, look, and listen for unique and repurposed furniture as you pass through your community. You may be surprised at the new treasures and creative ideas that will come to you.

## Repurposed Treasures

Classroom furniture should reflect the uniqueness of the teacher and students. Inviting spaces such as coffee shops, spas, and restaurants cater to their customer. Many places, like Starbucks, turn their spaces into major components of their brand. Anyone can do that and learn to make a space *pop!* Repurposed and inexpensive furniture can help create unique, inviting, and branded learning spaces. Look for ways to do that; you'll find them.

Adding simple chairs, stools, couches, covered milk crates, and various garage sale pieces can bring an alternative to traditional educational furniture. Pull padding and fabric over a two-foot by six-foot strip of plywood, place it over crates, and *voila!* An instant seat with storage space.

Large tires, cleaned up and painted bright colors, with cushions and pillows inside, offer unique places to sit. My students loved those creative, inviting seating options.

One middle school teacher created a space with a small reading lamp, coffee table, and two chairs, along with a small tabletop fountain and a bonsai tree, in a corner of her classroom. That provided a small Zen garden where anyone could relax as needed. I've seen a high school math teacher add a director's chair at the side of the room next to a dry erase board. That served as a teaching spot and focal area for his and his students' use at any time.

Another middle school teacher's room featured an outdoor patio set, complete with umbrella, in a corner in the learning space. Seventh graders enjoyed a discussion about the effect of the moon on the earth's tides while easily able to imagine they were sitting by the waves.

A simple clear shower curtain suspended from a tension rod in the ceiling near a corner of the room can create an impromptu conference space boundary.

### Kitchen and Bedroom Furniture

Where do most people gather in a house during the holidays? The kitchen. Where do most people go to relax and recharge? The bedroom. Use furniture from those two rooms to create gathering, relaxing, and thinking spaces for your classroom. Consider other home furniture as alternative seating and workspace options for your classroom.

When a teacher named Mary bought new dining furniture for her home, she brought her old kitchen table and four chairs to school. They became conferencing space for her class. She kept a vase of flowers atop the checkered tablecloth, just as she did at her home. The furniture gave her students a warm and homey atmosphere. That table and chairs—because they were residential furniture, not institutional—lent a familial atmosphere to the class, a place to gather or have a cookie. And that increased the value of each voice. I loved sitting there, too.

Imagine a high school drama teacher who wants to create magical, innovative nooks for her students. On the outside perimeter of the room, she marks off squares large enough to provide space for four people. Then she hangs rods holding clear or colored drop cloths, curtains, or beads. These areas house stools and other various types of seating, as well as scene props that would otherwise be kept in the school's storage closet. These nooks give students space for improv and scene practice. The remaining classroom space can be arranged as theater seating or for other uses as needed. The same can be done for a tech class, like adding displays of student-created furniture to then use as meeting spaces: stools, bookcases, lamps, or benches. Ask the family and consumer sciences teachers to design and make cushions for the benches, or curtains for the drama room.

○ **TEACHER TIP:**
Remember, garage sales almost always include used furniture. You can snatch it up *inexpensively* for your classroom. Sometimes if you explain why you want it, the owner will donate it to your classroom.

○ **TEACHER TIP:**
Remember to bring uniqueness to your space when searching for treasures; students will love the effort and the effect. STOP. LOOK. LISTEN. You can sometimes discover inexpensive futons, bunk beds, dressers, and bedroom desks as alternate classroom workspaces. When you stop for garage sales, flea markets, or even antique shops, think creatively about what you see. It may surprise you to see what you can do with what you come across. Place these new pieces in corners of the room use them to create nooks. Consider placing plants by pieces of furniture to create inviting places to work. Your students will love you for the effort.

## It's Not a Bathtub Anymore

Outdoor or indoor playtime tools can become stimulating learning spaces. Small, molded plastic swimming pools, beach chairs, and umbrella tables work well as gather-and-gab spots. It also helps to place them in ways that balance the room. I found a plastic rowboat with two oars one summer and brought it into my classroom to create a relaxing island of learning. These innovative spaces not only help students engage in learning, they also make the environment more fun and cozy. Imagine a lanky six-foot-three high school junior sitting, legs over the side of a bathtub, studying for a unit test.

○ **TEACHER TIP:**
The very act of offering seating options adds a spark to learning environments.

○ **TEACHER TIP:**
If you prefer a certain type of seating, table, or supply, try to add it to your classroom space. Whether a tractor stool, kitchen table, or an unusual clipboard, adding something you love will inspire your students as well. That makes learning more fun for everyone.

## Tables and Work Surfaces

Chairs are one of the essentials for civilization in homes, offices, and restaurants, in transit, and in the classroom. People typically either sit or stand to work, eat, drink, think, relax, and travel.

Horizontal services—think dining tables, counters, desks, airline seatback trays, and work benches—are almost equal to chairs in importance. Now,

Here is one table I used in my classroom, surrounded by camp chairs. Placing a plant on a table makes the area more welcoming.

think of the twentieth century's revolution in office space that transitioned from desks to "work surfaces." The old, boxy, seven-drawer steel desk gave way to an explosion of new designs of materials, shapes, and colors for corporate America. Who knew accountants, lawyers, architects, designers, secretaries, and executives wanted greater variety and utility in the flat or tilted surfaces that helped them create and manage?

A couple decades later, a similar upheaval came to classroom furniture. Some of that revolution was "prototyped" by inventive teachers like me who scrounged around through garage sales,

73

antique shops, and our own attics for old pieces we could turn to new purposes. Besides chairs and tables and bookshelves, we saw old bulletin boards, bathtubs, barrels, dressers, patio sets, porch rockers, area rugs, tool chests, saddles, and various dusty treasures morph into magical new roles in the lives of students. The building's storage closet can be a treasure trove for abandoned items other teachers no longer want in their rooms.

Over the years, I found folding camp chairs for sale, stools from garage sales, regular desks and tables with the legs lowered, and other treasures. They all provided unusual, fun, and alternative seating. In classrooms with older students and bigger bodies moving around, any furniture I could find that was easily moved, folded, and stored was a game-changer. Even replacing two or three tables and chairs with easily movable pieces makes a big impact on a space. I learned that it isn't always necessary to provide tables or desks for students' laptops. Many of my students preferred the folding camp chairs, placing their laptops in their laps. For those wanting a workspace, foldable or stackable tables were perfect for their needs and for easy storage. It can also be helpful to build a shelf at bar height along a wall where students can stand and work. That can eliminate three or four desks, freeing up more floor space. Think of it as an Apple store's Genius Bar.

### The Problem with *My* Desk

I watched my classroom become like a great train station, students passing through on their way to various learning destinations. Our space hummed with activity and purpose. But I slowly began to realize that while I had worked hard to provide sufficient and flexible furniture for my students, I hadn't paid enough attention to *my* desk. It was a relic, a steam locomotive on its last journey down the tracks, ready for abandonment.

I realized that the larger my desk, the less room was available for the students. Why did I need so much desk space? Since I constantly moved around the room, did I really benefit from such a large base station? Was my desk a relic I hung onto for reasons that didn't exist anymore? Was it purely sentimental? Finally, I did it: I took a risk, removed my immense desk, and brought in a smaller one from home.

My small desk still took too much space, especially with the bookshelves behind it. Had I really downsized? No. I realized I had just moved items around. So, I replaced the three bookshelves with two soft swivel chairs and a bistro table to provide another cozy learning nook. Then I downsized again, trading my desk for a podium on wheels.[4]

Switching to this smaller desk was an improvement, but it, and the bookshelves behind it, still took up too much space.

The movable podium held my laptop, document camera, and a workbook. It also held a small locking supply cabinet. I found a new level of freedom and flexibility by rolling the podium anywhere in the room. Perhaps best of all, my footprint became smaller than the student workspaces. By eliminating my "teacher needs" and making their workspace larger, I prioritized their learning over my space. I no longer kept my

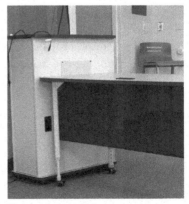

The switch to this moveable podium gave me more freedom and flexibility.

stuff spread out like a corporate CEO with acres of desk space.

Rather than feeling like I was losing something, though, I gained new freedom that meant I could teach and work anywhere in the room.

○ **TEACHER TIP:**
Inexpensive and repurposed items can transform a space with little investment. The revised space will give students room to breathe, rest, and focus.

○ **TEACHER TIP:**
Consider downsizing your teacher desk. Doing so will provide more freedom for you than you realize. That one small change gives the students permission to downsize their supplies, too.

### What I Hear as a Consultant

Today, I work as a consultant with K-12 schools. I often come up against the challenges inherent in years of tradition, and traditional furniture. That is especially true when I talk about the teacher desk issue. I get it. I know walking down an unknown path is scary. But let's face it: Classroom furniture should be more about function than personal identity. Plus, I found its removal to be invigorating and liberating! Less was more. I took a risk and discovered in that risk I could be a better teacher when I no longer clung to furnishings that made me appear as the supreme ruler over my students.

Some teachers ask where I graded papers or performed other teacher work if not at a desk. Wherever I sat became my workstation, whether the students were in class or not. I often sat at the couch or chair or stood at a tall table to do my work, all of which were inviting spaces for me. In removing the desk, I gave myself permission to do my teacher work anywhere in the room. That simple move allowed me to taste the same freedom the students feel when they move around freely.

Bins to collect papers—by subject, grade level, or class hour— were my go-to in organization. I had these before I downsized my personal workspace. They sat on top of a moving cart or countertop for the students and were labeled for easy access. I placed graded work in the bottom of each basket or bin, face down, for returning to students.

When I consult with them, I suggest to teachers that they move the teaching platform, small group gathering table, or downsized teacher desk to the middle of the room. This gives students the opportunity to tune into the instruction within small groups or as a whole class.

Sylvia, a middle school teacher I supported as a consultant, was reluctant to do that, but agreed to give it a shot. She then arranged student furniture around her teaching platform. She could easily reach twelve students when she taught small groups, and the entire room was in her line of sight. Soon after my visit, she emailed me to let me know she and her students loved the room change. They enjoyed the configuration's new access to the teacher and other students.

### What's a Coffee Shop Without Food?

I and most of my students loved animal crackers. I usually bought them in large plastic bins. We also loved Life Saver mints and popcorn! When someone gave me an old-fashioned popcorn machine, I used it in my classroom, treating students with the hot, buttery treat. They could smell it throughout the building before they even entered the room. Before long, I learned to make extra containers for my teaching teammates and the office staff as they began migrating to my room for popcorn! A classroom should be fun, like a coffee shop.

The coffee shop atmosphere was a success. My students enjoyed snacks while actively leaning into their learning. My fifth graders even bet on which class consumed the most mints in an academic year. With a single bag holding 500 pieces, one class polished off eight bags—or 4,000 mints. We never had a problem with bad breath!

I realize this may not be an option for many teachers today. Always ask your administration about the guidelines for food and drinks in classrooms.

⚙ **TEACHER TIP:**
If a total downsizing of your teacher workspace seems like too much, start small. Just change one section of your room at a time. Start by identifying what is essential. Once you've done that, ask if those essentials must remain on your desk. Do you really need 1,000 markers, sticky notes, erasers, and note paper? Can you eliminate half the supplies? Could your teacher space hold only your computer, document camera, and one small bucket of pens? The freedom you gain through keeping things simple may surprise you.

⚙ **TEACHER TIP:**
Supplies include both teacher and student items, classroom common supplies, and specific learning task materials. Think about which supplies are needed daily, weekly, or as a one-time necessity. Then create space for these items as you plan the use of the physical space.

# CHAPTER 8

# NUDGING THE LEARNING ENVIRONMENT

**A NUDGE IS OFTEN ALL IT TAKES TO MAKE A GOOD CHOICE EASIER AND A BAD CHOICE HARDER.**
**–Rex Miller–**[5]

In 1984, my first year of teaching, I walked into my career equipped with nothing but traditional methods and philosophies. I started out already wanting to break with the very past that had trained me. I represented the classic story of the new kid in town, impatient with the past and reaching for new possibilities.

I decided to inaugurate my bold new career through a move into the future. I adopted a class pet.

A student gave us a teddy bear hamster and the supplies to raise him. I agreed to keep it on the condition that someone would take him home over the summer. When my sixth graders volunteered to care for him, I bought a plastic hamster ball so he could roll around the classroom to his little heart's content.

Then one afternoon, we forgot about him. Before we realized he was gone, we heard a thump, followed by rolling sounds, then a loud crash! Two students rushed from the classroom to the scene of the accident. Soon the two came back with the hamster, slightly dazed from his roll across the building and his tumble down a flight of steps that had culminated in landing at the door leading to a busy road outside. Luckily, that door was shut! I guess he just wanted a taste of freedom.

The hamster experience taught me something: Space is important. We all naturally interact with our built environments —walls, floors, doors, ceilings, and windows. That's why we have architects. And just like the hamster, students needed to move freely into, within, and out of classrooms.

That hamster awareness dawned very simply when I noticed that many classrooms leave space along the walls so students can line up in straight lines to leave the room.

Why?

Do educators believe students will not know how to exit if they don't do so in a straight line? Early on, I did that in my classroom, too. What a waste of valuable learning space! Might there be alternate options for moving through our space in orderly ways? I thought so. I started with the students closest to the door and linked each cluster of students into the whole line. That meant students must notice when it was their turn to join the process. Yes, that's a simple maneuver, but it helped us reclaim wasted space for education and it saved me from constantly reminding students how to line up. Forward thinking creates forward movement. When I taught older students, I didn't need to think about this as I gave them permission to move when the end of period bell rang.

○ **TEACHER TIP:**
Think about rhythms and routines. Is there anything small you can tweak to streamline your class routines—roll call, supply collections, etc.?

## Lifeless Zones

As a teaching consultant, many rooms I visit contain underused and neglected areas. They are usually in a back corner and hold unused furniture, equipment, and junk. What wasted and ugly places! Light doesn't even reach those spots till the end of the school year when custodians move things around to clean. That's when they find loose change, pencil stubs, papers, dead bugs, fuzz balls, and maybe even one dead hamster. But every area in a classroom is full of potential. The entire space is important and should look valued and cared for.

I encourage teachers to try turning neglected corners into science exploration stations, math investigation corners, or maker spaces. Toss the old and create a new and inviting space. Design something that will draw students in. In one eighth grade classroom, a teacher created an electronics corner housing a pegboard wall of tools and movable carts of materials. The teacher added a laminate board and two shelves to showcase student work at each grade level. This became a place to see what the older grades were doing, and the display gave the younger students in the building something to look forward to.

Let's look at some classroom spaces that need to be revitalized with new purpose.

## Corners

According to Rex Miller,

> A nudge makes the right thing easy. It tips the better choice into the "automatic" realm. A fuel efficiency gauge near the speedometer is a nudge toward slower and gentler driving. Displaying bottled water and healthy juices at convenient reach (and hiding soft drinks) nudges people toward healthier consumption.[6]

The same thing applies to classrooms. For example, think of the boring bookshelves you probably remember from your K-12 classrooms. Reading corners were likely crammed into tiny spots, abandoned and neglected. That is no way to promote a love of books and reading.

Tucking learning nooks away from inquiring minds seems to say, *DO NOT TOUCH unless the teacher invites you*. That placement does not promote exploration or curiosity. But hands-on work centers—the sensory table, block building station, and a rocking chair with books—invite students to dive into the work at hand. The same would work wonderfully in a middle school setting. Imagine erector sets on tables for middle schoolers to explore as they design a new bridge for their school's pond. Just bring the materials to class, then allow students of all ages to explore.

Let's imagine: What would happen if a science classroom contained bookshelves in various shapes, soft seating, stools, magnifying glasses, measuring squares or triangles, tape measures, or test tubes throughout the space, with supplies stored in bins on the floor for easy and inviting access? When it comes to literacy, what if a teacher released students to create book posters or online projects to promote favorite books or authors, which their peers could later view by scanning QR codes hanging from the ceiling to open each project? A similar method could be used to view student-generated how-to videos about the Pythagorean theorem, the periodic table, US and world economics, a *Harry Potter* book review, a summary of the Egyptian Empire, and more.

Upscale bookstores invite customers to read novels and play games throughout the store. They even add high-quality and comfortable chairs and sofas. Barnes and Noble is happy to let shoppers pull books from shelves and sit and read with a cup of coffee, perhaps gaining a sale or two. Could education learn something from that approach? Could we promote a love of science, history, math, and more by bringing these approaches to exploration directly into the learning space?

○ **TEACHER TIP:**
Think of the tasks students will be doing. Then make sure the room supports them in its physical layout and visual appeal.

○ **TEACHER TIP:**
Remember, whatever you create and optimize in your corner areas should be as riveting and valuable as what's in the center of the classroom.

## Live Plants

I once had a huge Boston fern in my room. As I watered and misted it every day, it wasn't long before it took over, reminding me of the plant Audrey from the movie *Little Shop of Horrors*. Thankfully, my fern didn't eat anyone.

We sometimes think of plants as delicate creatures. But they often do some heavy lifting in the design of educational spaces. They help create cozy and inviting spaces, serve as space partitions, bring the outdoors into the classroom, and call students to care for other life forms. Live plants give the atmosphere several nudges toward better learning.

○ **TEACHER TIP:**
Arrange for students to visit a local nursery. They might even ask the nursery for a donation of small starter plants. Then give students the responsibility to care for them. Student groups can create plant journals. Each year a new team of botanists can continue a tradition that can build a legacy for future classes. They can even give the plants to local stores or senior centers as gifts if the students think that's a good idea. Begin with new starter plants the following year.

○ **TEACHER TIP:**
Consider adding a grow light with trays for seedlings,

small plastic terrariums, or even an ant farm, to your room. Live plants (or other inhabitants!) really do add dimension and wonder to the learning space.

## Silk Trees

Silk trees provide the same benefits as other trees, but without the watering. I once had six, six-foot-tall silk trees in my classroom. Hanging small strands of white lights on each further transformed the learning space. I placed one tree next to my rocking chair, which, combined with a large area rug, created a very comfy gathering place. We moved the silk trees around to create unique spaces and soft barriers throughout the year.

## Academic and Content-Specific Spaces

Transforming familiar learning spaces and nooks into unfamiliar locales is a great way to spur creativity and curiosity. One of my former students, Suzie, is now a biomedical engineer who worked on a lead team to find a vaccine for COVID-19. She recently told me by email that she enjoyed the learning experiences and spaces I provided. Perhaps our classroom nudges inspired a future biomedical engineer!

Suzie especially liked one event I created, the "Iditikid" experience. After studying the Iditarod, the long-distance sled dog race in Alaska, I incorporated all academic subjects into the study while we tracked the race progress. For each lesson, I determined the best student groupings and furniture arrangements. I arranged formative and summative assessments, checkpoints, quizzes, and student reflections on my unit calendar to track progress. One glance told me when I needed to pull small groups, introduce new lessons, or offer extension work for those excelling and support those needing extra help.

That unit brought the faraway sporting event to life for the students. As a concluding activity, I developed several hour-long Iditikid races around the school grounds. We placed students into triad sled teams along a predetermined route from "Anchorage" to "Nome." At one stop, a guest from our Colorado park and recreation district spoke about layering clothing in cold weather. Another station featured a nurse who spoke about frostbite. Another guest explained how to identify flora in the area. The supply station gave students the challenge of loading their sleds with actual supplies. I asked the father of one of our students to teach us how to use a compass. Another station demonstrated how to set up a tent and build a fire. A local sled dog sprint racer brought her dog and racing sled to the school and explained the unique challenges of that sport.

To top off the morning, we held a ceremony at the Nome finish line, complete with medals and a treat. That race still stands as a lesson on how to transform a mundane physical space into an exotic learning adventure. In an environment with older students, middle schoolers and high schoolers could focus on one aspect of the race. Science and math classes could examine the effect of weather on the sleds. High schoolers could analyze the racecourse for the four types of slopes. Whether you have a day or two or an entire week, moving furniture and thinking creatively about these kinds of projects immerses students in one or more aspects of learning.

One nudge that influenced me came when I was in high school. My Shakespearean literature class was set inside a replica of Shakespeare's Globe Theatre! Our teacher's desk sat on the large stage. From our student desks and chairs, placed on three different tiers, we enjoyed the teacher's performance of the greatest Shakespeare scenes. For the forty-five-minute class, I could almost believe I was observing history from my top row, left side seat. That nudge made Shakespeare come alive for me and many others. Indulge in your own forward thinking and you'll be surprised what can develop.

**⚙ TEACHER TIP:**
Think fresh when adding specific elements to the classroom. Consider scaling an item to make it ten times larger than its actual size, creating a larger-than-life mural on an entryway into the classroom. Or, physically mount a collection of old cameras on a classroom wall near the school's photo lab. Build shelves on a wall in a science room to hold displays of test tubes. These visuals support the creation of a more themed learning space. Ask students to paint an original mural depicting places, themes, or scenes onto classroom walls, hallways, or large gathering places. Draw them into the learning environment with color and images. Classrooms don't have to be pedantic or somber. A sense of whimsy is always welcome and appreciated.

## Lesson Development

As a teacher and as a consultant, I've learned that classroom furniture is a part of the total package. I still ask questions as a consultant that I first asked as a teacher:

1. How should the room be rearranged for a specific educational purpose?

2. What is that purpose?

3. How will the students use this space?

4. Will students work in pairs, small groups, or rotating stations?

5. What technology will we use?

6. What materials will we need?

7. How much freedom of movement can we create?

I also consider the learning tasks and state standards as we match furniture to needs. For example, if we are working in a science lab, I may place tables of varying heights in the center of the room.

We all know the huge role technology plays in education today. The more technology becomes prevalent in learning, the more creative teachers must be to increase students' interactive and interpersonal skills. Teachers must include more human aspects to learning however and whenever possible. In addition to the standards and technology, the furniture must always support the task. Function follows form.

○ **TEACHER TIP:**
Don't forget that classroom walls, doors, and floors also represent prime learning territory. They too should nudge students in the right direction. For example, inspiring and positive quotes on walls and doors nudge students into proper attitudes and thinking.

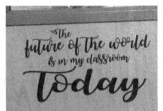

Inspiring words can influence students and nudge them in the right direction for learning, growth, and positivity.

## Functional Wall Art

Business, education, restaurant, and retail spaces carefully plan everything that hangs on their walls. Their wall art supports their function. In the same way, bulletin boards, quotations, displays, maps, charts, and color must be considered when decorating the learning environment. All "functional wall art," to use the term I coined for education, should draw the eye into new worlds and thoughts. Color coordinated spaces will present a clean, organized, focused, and professional appearance. Remember that wood, fabric, and metal bring richness and texture to the room (and don't fade or deteriorate as quickly as paper). We do not want to create visual pollution.

My husband and I created the wall sculpture shown for my classroom. It represents my view that wall art should add real dimension and love of knowledge to the space. This hanging spurred discussions of radius and circumference.

## Focus

When you walk into a classroom, can you easily and quickly detect the purpose of the room? Consider the furniture and furnishings, watch how students move and interact within that space, and study what adorns the walls. Does it all work together to support specific learning purposes? Math and science require more space for materials, experiments, and research. That usually translates into a need for hard surfaces—lots of banging, breaking, and spilling! Reading- and writing-focused environments need soft furniture, organized in small groupings, as well as tables and storage for books and print materials, writing dialogues, and poetry slams. Just like commercial space, the decor and ambience of educational space should immediately establish the tone and focus for the room.

> ○ **TEACHER TIP:**
> To add zest to your room, consider adding a signature piece of furniture or a wall piece. Make your room stand out as it sends a message of care and style to the students.

## Windows!

Most of the schools in history were built in a utilitarian, economical, and boring style. That usually meant no or very small windows. Thankfully, most twenty-first-century school architecture includes generous windows. Everyone loves classrooms with windows. They pull our eyes outward to the larger world. Windows also bring weather and nature into the learning space, and nature relaxes the soul. Windows can also enhance and integrate the room's functional wall art. Notice how the windows in the following photo support the cowboy hats.

And that was important: Each hat represented a story, our story. Every year my students were proud to take ownership of it, sharing and listening to others, adding to the legacy.

Research confirms what we all know: windows give the best lighting for learning. But for those classrooms that lack natural lighting (from windows or skylights), lamps are great alternatives and can add to the ambience. Many new or remodeled schools utilize mood lighting, which allows the color spectrum and intensity to change based on the learning need. Bottom line: Lighting—whether natural, lamps, or mood lighting—should be seen as pivotal to learning.

In a slightly related topic, teachers should consider adding accent wall colors to classroom learning space. Like mood lighting, accent colors can also support attitudes conducive to learning. In my final classroom, the accent wall color was green. I chose it to obscure the view of the parking lot. The green walls helped to pull the trees beyond the parking lot and along the neighbors' fences into the room. Students looked past the asphalt and cars to see the glory of nature and the beauty of every season.

○ **TEACHER TIP:**
Ever consider painting a large "window" or mural on a wall? It can open the door to creativity! The wardrobe from the Narnia series would be a perfect backdrop in a literature-focused space!

## Wall Boards

I also used a variety of wall boards to support a learning atmosphere. To do that, I had to consider the best ways to meet educational needs through the placement, size, and functions of bulletin boards and dry erase boards.

In the photo above, the small squares are individual, removable dry erase squares. Bulletin boards and magnetic boards like the ones above can be hung at various heights for different purposes. The wall boards bring the walls into full partnership, just like furniture and lighting, in supporting learners. Everything placed on the walls should be done with purpose. Intentionally designed spaces demand that floors and walls be consistent with the learning needs of the classroom. Posters hung haphazardly do not promote learning. Clutter distracts students. Too much of what adorns classroom walls does not serve students; posters and other graphics only hide the staples or nail holes inflicted over the years.

Placement of furnishings and decor depends on the ages or grades of the learners who meet in that space. Naturally, young students need surfaces that start at the floor. Older students can utilize surfaces mounted higher, even ones that extend from floor to ceiling.

**✿ TEACHER TIP:**
Consider the instructional purpose and learner age and grade when determining wall use.

**✿ TEACHER TIP:**
When placing boards on the wall, try hanging them in different directions or angles. Getting away from the grid appearance invites the eye to dance between different shapes.

## Hallways
In addition to their primary purpose of facilitating student movement and storage, hallways can and should increase the atmosphere of learning.

For example, my teammates and I allowed our students to develop, collect, and display a living history museum in the hallways at the end of the academic year. They designed it as an interactive display and testament to their learning. Each part of the display identified and described the artifact and the contributor. The hallway walls extended our voices far beyond our classroom.

**✿ TEACHER TIP:**
Today, many schools incorporate common spaces for a pod or cluster of classrooms. Think of these as extensions of the classroom; they are not just spaces where kids can work quietly out of sight. These spaces are designed to allow greater student interaction. Think of the shared spaces as opportunities to enrich the learning. Invite other grade levels or disciplines to interact there.

**✿ TEACHER TIP:**
The hallway should be an extension of the learning space. Mark off large squares outside the classroom door, presenting them as something like "indoor patios." Students can reserve these spaces, moving folding camp

chairs or cushions to the spots. Provide fun, inexpensive lanterns or other related theme items for them.Learning can now happen in these spots that were once considered simply "the hallway" but are now "the patio," "nook," or "garden." A small plant can be placed in each area. If possible, set up similar zones outside.

## Area Rugs

Area rugs help define and anchor learning spaces. They also contribute to the visual cohesion of the room. Rugs serve as islands of humanity in a sea of industrial-grade carpet or linoleum.

**⚙ TEACHER TIP:**
Individual carpet squares can also define workspaces. Ask carpet stores for their outdated samples. Place them in key locations throughout the room. Students can grab one and work wherever they like.

## Charts

Most classrooms include charts. But unless they are well-designed and placed, they can create visual pollution. I relocated all charts in my classrooms to a moveable display stand.

I discovered it helped to use various sizes and colors of charts for easier student reference. So, I laminated charts I knew I'd need, especially those presenting students' work as exemplars.

**⚙ TEACHER TIP:**
Remember that charts serve the purpose of instruction. If students can write and display their work on charts and create the how-tos, their learning goes much further as they teach others. Think of electronic charts, too. Use QR codes to showcase students work and instruction. Middle and high schoolers can create QR codes to announce upcoming school plays, sports, student government activities, and clubs. Build student agency organically and watch it flourish.

# CHAPTER 9

# PUTTING THE PIECES TOGETHER

Commercial, public-use, and other enclosed or outdoor spaces invite people to enter and enjoy everything within. Such spaces might offer a special coffee of the week, a holiday pie on the menu, athletic facilities, a movie, or a hot-air balloon ride. When we relax or work in these spaces, we join something special. We walk away better than we were before we got there. And we know we will return.

Twenty-first century classroom designs and furniture can achieve the same effect. That's why students—from kindergarten through college—find well-designed educational spaces uplifting and empowering. They feel the energy to work and thrive in those spaces the moment they walk into them. Those spaces give life. I kept that in mind as I created learning spaces, trying to create transformative experiences that would extend beyond our room's physical footprint.

## Curriculum, Standards, and Authentic Experiences

*Why do we have to learn this?* Teachers hear that question frequently from students. And I understand why they ask. Why do we keep doing the same language arts, science, or math units over and over? Teachers ask variations of the same question.

At some point, those questions made me realize something was missing from my instruction. As I reflected further, I saw the need to build hands-on, authentic learning opportunities around real-life problems. Naturally, my teaching had to support state standards and curricular objectives, and I also needed to continue pushing the boundaries on procuring furniture that would best support the work. To get started, I developed a template to ensure I had all the components for this new learning mode (more on that later).

## Beds for Barks

To explore a new learning mode, I merged language arts and math into a new educational opportunity. My students would design and build pet beds for the local humane society or for families in need. Weekly lesson plans revolved around the skills they'd need. Through small group and whole group instruction, we created checkpoints for student understanding of the skills, extension and support work, student reflections, and final presentations. The classroom furniture morphed into new arrangements as our room became a bed research station and assembly line. We measured, requested material from local fabric stores and lumber yards, designed prototypes, and then built the beds. We even posted pictures of our pets on the wall as a reminder of the clients we were serving.

Something about building a real-world product created an invested workforce. I could see this fresh approach even carried the potential of helping students better understand the principles and dynamics behind a market economy. Learning came more naturally and enthusiastically with the emotional connection to solving real-world needs. Students could relate to that in a very primary and personal way. Who doesn't want to see a cute puppy or kitten enjoying a new bed?

○ **TEACHER TIP:**
Is there a local zoo or park nearby that could benefit from a student project?

## Oil Spill

With the success of the Beds for Barks unit, I knew I could and must create student empathy for problems beyond our local view. For example, how could we build a visceral connection to the use and abuse of our planet's natural resources?

To create that emotional connection, we brought the problem of an oil spill right into our classroom. That was one day's

lesson, yet the impact it created was worth a week's worth of work or online tech videos. I wrote the standard they were to learn on the board and how it was to be measured. Then I rearranged the furniture to represent an oil spill investigation and cleanup site. I wanted the room to look as authentic as possible. Each student received secret files of information about the spill as they worked to solve the problem. For background knowledge, we watched several video clips from *National Geographic* on various resources and their uses in our planet. The immersive and applicable experience came next. The room became our ocean as we rescued birds (feathers)

Rearranging furniture and adding decorative elements like caution tape brought our oil spill unit to life.

from the oil (cocoa powder mixed with oil and water) using only cotton balls, cotton swabs, and paper towels. We came away with new knowledge of specific science, math, and language arts standards. And it was all driven by solving a real-life problem. The activity was only forty-five minutes in length. My cleanup at the end of the day took a few hours, but it was worth the extra time!

Placing students into an authentic problem and giving them room to investigate, communicate, and collaborate had results that reached deeper and wider than I expected.

The students talked about their work for days. Some wanted to take action to support real cleanups in our area, all because they found real traction in processes and outcomes through our oil cleanup simulation. If any former students become involved in environmental activism, we may discover that some part of their inspiration goes back to an aluminum pan filled with oil, water, cocoa powder, and coated feathers.

> ⚙ **TEACHER TIP:**
> Try planning one curricular unit a trimester or a month to start. I was always surprised at the level of excitement and love of learning that planning produces in students.

### Unit and Lesson Plan Template

To expand on that approach, I created a template to capture all the pieces—the best furniture configuration, student needs, state standards, ways for students to demonstrate mastery of subjects, group dynamics, and other planning lenses. These are in the Appendices section of this book.

To further illustrate this point, when planning group dynamics with curriculum, I considered the task and the ability of every student. Then I placed them into groups of comparable (or sometimes opposite) abilities. I also arranged the furniture to suit the project. After assigning students to groups, they determined where in the room they wanted to work. I watched group dynamics and communication skills become more authentic and effective. For example, the class worked through points of view in primary sourced Revolutionary War documents about the Boston Tea Party. The students' writing and comprehension abilities determined their work level for the task. They had to determine whose point of view interpreted the evidence and offer support for their position. So, we arranged the furniture into quaint alcoves and niches for groups of four students each. Groups had to collectively decide which niche they wanted, considering each person's learning inclination from the class preference chart. The student groupings and furniture nudged them to work together.

## Pizza Boxes: Circular Nudges in High School Geometry

I learned if I created a unit that involved real world application for a dry concept, such as natural resources, students would become more engaged. For another example, if you want to promote understanding of the arc of a circle, bring in something that catches high schoolers' attention: pizza!

Watch them collect protractors, compasses, rulers, and local restaurants' small pizza boxes to determine which restaurant has the most crust in a small pizza. Place materials on a round table nearby and provide room to measure plastic circles, pie tins, pie plates, pizza boxes, and anything cylindrical. Arrange the tables into circular configurations so students can find the arc of the classroom's physical shape. To conclude the activity, bring in real pizza to hold a fun taste test upon unit completion.

In my lesson plan template that follows, I've given a basic understanding of each day's lessons, student groupings, and checkpoints. The codes in each box represent assessments, teacher lessons, and the physical room arrangement. The coding helped me to design quality lessons with an intentional plan for the environment and student experiences. I adjusted my

## Sample Lesson Plan

| Monday | Tuesday | Wednesday |
|--------|---------|-----------|
| ◌ Unit Introduction: Day 1 and ◎ Preassessment <br><br> ⬤ **Whole Huddle** (12) then **Retreat Bungalows**, for preassessment | ⬤ **Retreat Bungalows** (1) to establish individual learning goals | ⬤ **Exploration Stations** (2 or 7) to discover individual learning focus preferences for a project or task <br><br> ◌ Teacher 1:1 conferences to discuss student learning goals |
| ◎ Entrance ticket #2 **Retreat Bungalows** (1) then ⬤ **Convene Ravines** (3 or 8) <br><br> ◌ Teacher support based on entrance tickets "look over" | ◌ Teacher focused small group support, based on yesterday's entrance tickets <br><br> ⬤ **Convene Ravines** (3 or 8) and ◌ Student-led small group teaching (5) | ◌ Teacher anecdotal note taking on students <br><br> ⬤ **Convene Ravines** (3 or 8) or **Exploration Stations**, based on group needs |
| ⬤ **Convene Ravines** (2) or ⬤ **Exploration Stations** (3) with furniture arranged into 6 groups | ◌ Teacher small group support lessons to check student progress <br><br> ⬤ **Exploration Stations** (8 or 11) | ⬤ **Exploration Stations** (8 or 11) or ⬤ **Convene Ravines** (8 or 11) <br><br> ◎ Whole class exit ticket #3 |
| ◎ Entire class quiz <br><br> ⬤ **Retreat Bungalows** (1) to assess and reflect on learning progress before final mastery demonstrations and assessment | ◌ Teacher lesson: final wrap-up <br><br> ⬤ **Whole Huddle** (12) | ⬤ **Retreat Bungalows** (1) for final preparation, reflections |

| | | |
|---|---|---|
| ◌ | Teacher lesson: group or 1:1 support or extension Students teaching others as well | ⬤ Physical Room Arrangement Taxonomy –see Appendix C pages 120-121 for specifics on each arrangement |

**Retreat Bungalows**: Opportunities for students to singly process, work, and restore.

**Convene Ravines**: Groups of 2-4 students communicating, collaborating, and using shared resources.

Numbers correlate with the Physical Room Arrangement Taxonomy in Appendix C

Additional ideas for learning spaces can be found in David Thornburg's book *From the Campfire to the Holodeck*.[8]

| Thursday | Friday |
|---|---|
| ◌ Teacher group lesson<br>● **Whole Huddle** (6 or 12)<br>● **Exploration Stations** (2 or 7), Day 2<br>◯ Exit ticket #1<br>● **Retreat Bungalows** (1) | ◌ Individual Student Work<br>● **Convene Ravines** (7) to collaboratively work from students' 2 days of self-exploring discoveries<br>◌ Teacher 1:1 conferences to discuss student learning |
| ● **Retreat Bungalows** (1) to reflect on learning goals progress<br>◯ Teacher quick check-ins (drive-bys) with anecdotal notes | ◌ Teacher whole group lesson #2<br>● **Whole Huddle** (4 or 6) |
| ◌ Teacher lesson, half of class<br>● **Convene Ravines** (8 or 11) or **Exploration Stations**<br>◌ Student-led small group teaching (4 or 10) | ◌ Teacher lesson, other half of class<br>● **Convene Ravines** (11) |
| ● **Convene Ravines** (7 or 8) for final focus group preparations & reflections<br>◌ Teacher final wrap-up **Whole Huddle** | ◯ Final assessment **Retreat Bungalows** (1)<br>● **Whole Huddle** (12) for student presentations (9) then<br>● **Convene Ravines** for group assessment and reflections of their work. |

| | |
|---|---|
| ◯ | Formal and Summative Assessment (entrance, exit tickets, quizzes, interviews, anecdotal records) |

**Exploration Stations:** Classroom spaces supporting student opportunities to manipulate and cocreate.

**Whole Huddle:** Classroom community-building spaces for whole group instruction, presentations, and student support. Many teachers also refer to this as Homebase.

instruction based on formative assessment results during the week. Entrance or exit tickets, teacher-student discussions, check-ins, and student work provided data to tailor instruction around my students' needs. I embedded a particular lesson from the textbook where I specifically taught from the text. Any slide decks, guest speakers, videos, or other tech were also included. A unit such as this might take a week or more depending on the content and time allotted in the year to teach the subject. The template allowed me to see everything I needed to know at a glance: teaching lessons, small group support, student assessments, group work time, and environmental design.

## Boxing Baseballs: Finding Area, Volume, and Perimeter

This unit was written for fifth graders and followed the teacher textbook math unit. In addition to the standard teacher lessons for finding the area, perimeter, and volume of the baseball boxes, I wanted a real-world aspect to the work to raise the level of student engagement using an interdisciplinary approach. I had them write to Major League baseball teams with questions about the number of baseballs they go through in a season. The specific question we addressed was simple: How were the baseballs packaged? What size containers were used for single and for multiple baseballs? Students organized into small groups to reach out to their favorite teams for that information. They also asked the teams to donate a baseball to our classes' investigative efforts.

The general manager of our state's baseball team replied to our questions with an official team response. He answered all our inquiries and sent an official baseball from the team. The kids were thrilled for such a kind and thorough response. We framed the letter and placed the baseball into a keepsake container. As far as we were concerned, the team hit it out of the ballpark for three classes of fifth grade students. The additional work of packaging the baseballs was included throughout the unit's lessons and served as a center for the research. Students responded because they could see the connections to the basic unit work they had to do each day. That brought the material to life.

Continuing in the baseball theme, I showed my students the classic Abbott and Costello skit, *Who's on First?* We used their opening lines as a banter between the class and myself when I wanted their attention.

The specific Boxing Baseballs unit was written out in the same format as the high school unit on the dimensions and geometry of pizza boxes. I've shown the basics of three weeks' work. I tracked student progress with the entrance and exit slips to determine small group support. Kids moved throughout the room as determined by either the lesson or task for the day. An observer would see hands-on, workbook, technology, teacher support, and research happening in the room each day. Sometimes the focus was a lesson and other times it was research and manipulation/hands-on experimentation. Whether a math, science, or literacy unit, the template allowed me to plug in the components to utilize the room with the lessons.

### Planning Template: Questions to Keep in Mind When Planning Any Unit

I created a template I used for planning a unit. It allowed me to see the work needed from an eagle's viewpoint a mile up.

I used a color-coded week or month calendar template that allowed me to view daily each component as it fit into my lessons. I could see at a glance my teaching focus days and the specific lesson, how the students would be grouped and their focus, any technology piece, and assessments.

I let the students understand their groupings for each day. That helped me keep track of locations and tasks. I displayed that on my front screen using a slide deck. Students could then move easily from area to area as we determined (as a group) where the tech area would be housed for the unit, while the hands-on area for building was in another location. My teaching spot could be in the center or at a side of the room, wherever I needed space to work with students. Movement and purpose drove each day's tasks. Students were equally invested, as they could see immediately when there would be check-ins or quizzes, group presentations, and final assessments.

### Completing Our 1,000-Mile Journey

The final "authentic teaching" unit of my career started in August 2018 and ended in May 2019. Ninety-three students at my grade level researched, designed, and built raised garden beds for our school. We reconfigured the classroom into the perfectly designed and furnished space for that project.

The students led the venture. They decided on the number of raised beds, shapes and configurations, location, contents, their care, and the legacy for future generations. They also created signage marking their legacy.

My teammates and I facilitated two student focus groups in our rooms every Wednesday. We saw them work toward a common goal while they learned valuable life skills. They faced challenges and setbacks, yet persevered through hard work and interaction with experts and school district personnel to find answers to their probing questions. They purchased materials in April and finished the project in early May. More than that, we watched them discover other students' strengths and find respect for students they had not known before the project. They knew their voices were heard and valued. Our classroom became a laboratory for a hands-on learning experience. The students also made the space their own. Our room seemed to breathe excitement and energy. The students owned their work and everything in the classroom on Wednesdays. They engaged the project as a collective whole. Even the shy, unengaged students, in their self-selected group, created work that was valued by their classmates. All voices were heard and honored.

The journey proved to be a great success.

## ✿ TEACHER TIP:

Releasing students to embrace a project that addresses authentic needs will build an experience they will not forget.

# CHAPTER 10

# NEXT STEPS

In *Seven Blind Mice* by Ed Young (Puffin Books, 2002), the title mice come across an enormous animal they cannot see. One by one each mouse scampers across different parts of the animal's body and returns to describe the strange creature to the others. Naturally, their descriptions paint the wrong picture. Finally, the seventh mouse goes to explore and figures out what the others missed.

Flexible seating and teaching can also turn into an adventure of seeing only parts of the whole. My journey into flexible seating and teaching took years of trial and error before I learned to see the whole picture, just as the seventh mouse did. I hope you will see all the pieces as they come together in your classroom. The materials in the appendices can support this work.

### Next Steps

As you stand in a new era of education, what is your next step? How are you going to make learning come alive in your flexible learning environment?

Are you ready to jump in? Will the environment you create be flexible enough for your students?

Let me suggest a few actionable steps to begin your classroom transformation.

## Step One: Mindset Shift

What do you see when you look at your classroom? Are your desks or tables in rows? Do you allow movement in your classroom?

What you allow in your classroom can inhibit students, or help them flourish. I know seating may seem like a minor issue. It isn't. Function follows form. Flexible seating can release curiosity in a child. Yes, it has the power to do that. That's why FLEX-ED is so important.

Classroom transformation usually starts with a teacher's mindset. Think about it: Education requires that minds change. Even though no one in college or grad school probably told you this, that change of mind always starts with you, the teacher. Face it: You will change your mind. Often. And your mindset exerts a powerful influence upon your students' learning.

This mindset power is evident in the pages of this book. The stories shared here came about because I and others saw inflexibility in the education system and decided to do something different. We didn't see ourselves as "change agents." But what we saw in the system began to impact us at an individual level. We felt it before we conceptualized it.

What was it that we felt? In his book, *WHOLE: What Teachers Need to Help Students Thrive*, Rex Miller recalls the words of Dr. Jeff Jernigan, who described burnout as "A thousand invisible betrayals of purpose that go unnoticed until it is too late."[7] Every teacher I've ever met knows those "thousand invisible betrayals of purpose." They exist because of a system that brings inflexibility to the wondrous job of teaching the young people of our society.

Through FLEX-ED, we are changing minds and bringing a human touch to that role. To accept change is the first and most powerful step.

## Step Two: Furniture

Many teachers tell me they struggle with classroom desks and tables. They cannot easily move those bulky pieces of furniture. So, think flexibly. If you're stuck in a twentieth-century classroom, with pieces of furniture as big as Buicks, can you still change your seating arrangement to better suit the learners?

You can allow students to sit on the carpet, to sit sideways in their desks, or to remove the legs from desks to change workspace or seating heights. You can also allow students to have floor space, modify desks for various heights, and give standing space for students.

Ask your students for help. Trust me; most can be very creative. Maybe they can help guide the next steps.

If your administration will allow you to get rid of desks, you can instead use tables, the tops of bookshelves, and other furniture. As you read in Chapter 4, I've built, borrowed, bought, or seen other teachers use new, even radical, alternatives in classroom furniture—tables, couches, a covered wagon, a bathtub, a treehouse, floor cushions, benches, beanbags, and pillows. Never be afraid to try new things.

○ **TEACHER TIP:**
It is important to document progress, challenges, and successes with every class project. Involve your students. Having some evidence of the learning for future generations captures the experience but, more importantly, provides a voice for the students and their impact made in the school or community. You never know when a student may rise to become a world changer from a simple project in your class.

### Step Three: Instruction

Does your instruction's attitude and practice include authentic, engaging activities?

Look for ideas and projects that require movement, inquiry, and collaboration. Find ways to teach that don't make you the sage on the stage. You'll find yourself more useful as a teacher when you coach or prompt students to discover or to increase their learning and curiosity through critical thinking. That approach leads to autonomy and maturity in a learner. You, as a teacher, should become one part of the collaborative curiosity.

### Step Four: Teacher Space

Does your teacher corner or desk take up a lot of space?

If so, that can send the message that the teacher controls the learning. The teacher guards the vault of knowledge. As a teacher and as a consultant, I've learned that a moveable workstation undercuts that image by allowing teachers to meet learners in their environment, at eye level. A teacher who constantly moves among the kids has broken open the four corners of the classroom. When that happens, students know you are accessible and that you learn with them.

### Step Five: The Learner

Do you allow your students to examine *how* they learn?

Questionnaires or informal surveys can help them. Students who discover their learning identity can better recognize how they learn best and where they need to push themselves. That intrinsic motivation can expand their learning stature and provide valuable self-reflection and growth.

### Step Six: Breaking the Walls of the Classroom

Does your classroom instruction allow students to see themselves as learners and citizens beyond the four walls of your space—locally, nationally, and globally? Does your leadership help them develop empathy for others?

I saw what happened when I helped students write letters to local businesses asking for funding for class projects. And I've seen students share in a way that brings awareness of important issues. That's why I've appointed student ambassadors for my classrooms. I saw that student leadership can encourage students to push themselves in many ways. When visitors stop in, student ambassadors introduce themselves, present learning tasks, and ask visitors to sign the guest book.

To help student leadership reach beyond the classroom walls, I once formed a partnership with Lockheed Martin and my elementary school. Each week, five aeronautical engineers dedicated a full afternoon to mentor my gifted and talented students. For five months, the group worked to build a three-dimensional model of an environment on the surface of Mars. The engineers used their experiences and expertise to support young minds as they thought beyond the classroom walls about how to improve the lives of others on our planet. These young voices gained even more strength later when they presented to the board of education in our district's central office.

Flexible environments bring the greatest impact when they lead to discovering within the school setting and beyond, engaging the wider community. This type of learning brings the world to life in ways kids and the community may never have experienced before. If you want to profoundly impact your students, just open the doors of your classroom and invite the world in. You never know what could happen.

○ **TEACHER TIP:**
Go big when looking for a unique partnership. There are others who will likely be eager to partner if approached. Research and reach out. You never know what might develop.

## CHAPTER 11

# YOUR JOURNEY

I hope you have picked up some ideas, nudges, and dreams for your classroom from these pages. As educators, we all want the best for our students. That's why I am passionate about flexible classroom environments. They help give students the voice, choice, and engagement necessary to manage their own learning. That is especially true when they step into a career.

Most teachers want to make a difference in the lives of students. We want to empower them to become contributing members of society. I feel the same; that's why I'm so committed to flexible seating and dynamic learning classrooms. Flexible environments have been proven to benefit a very diverse population of students. And flexible education increased my own joy, energy, and creativity for teaching. That is part of the value of a flexible approach; teacher growth expands right along with the kids' in *our* grand learning adventure.

And that's why I continue my passionate advocacy for flexible learning environments. But now I do so by supporting teachers through my consulting work. If you need a support partner, I suggest you contact:

MeTEOR Education
690 NE 23rd Ave • Gainesville, FL 32609
800-699-7516 • https://meteoreducation.com

They can contact me if you would like my help. Whether you are looking for the latest in the educational furniture MeTEOR provides or you're searching craft fairs and garage sales for furniture for your classroom, I can help. I've worked with flea market and garage sale furnishings and repurposed objects. And I've also worked with the best of the new and most innovative classroom furniture designs. I have learned that the creative spark is more important than the specific furniture. I have developed a process that supports the FLEX-ED mind shift necessary for the learning environments. It's so much more than simply placing "cool furniture" into a learning space.

My flexible seating classrooms provided not only a unique environment but a place where my students felt welcomed and loved. If my classroom and teaching styles changed the game for K-12 kids, then I accomplished what I set out to do: make a positive difference for their lives.

### Why Flexible Learning Environments?

We often use the term "ivory tower" as an academic reference, suggesting a place of elite reflections and esoteric pursuits; a tower of unreality that rises above life's hard truths. That may be why education often seems aloof toward business. Educators sometimes ignore or misunderstand the vital connection between learning and working.

But our contemporary economic life forces us to better understand the crucial connections between education and employment. This is partly why, just as offices and other workplaces have moved toward flexible environments, education must do the same. The skills, training, furniture, innovation, and collaboration are common to both. The better we become at providing flexible environments and practices in education, the better prepared our graduates will be for their future careers.

I once served as a member of my district's Innovative Champion Committee. Our committee focused on fostering new patterns of thinking in business and the connections between business and education. We studied physical workplace environments: cutting-edge gyms, conference nooks, adaptive technologies, open and inviting kitchens, large and small gathering rooms, flexible clusters used as work areas, and many other new forms of flexibility in the workplace. In every business we studied, we interviewed employees about the environments and the skills or experiences essential to entering the workforce.

Every employee we talked with, from the CEO to the newest worker, addressed the importance of the following point in the work world today:

1. Many businesses are changing physical layouts to better accommodate the changing needs around work. Today's workplace may see various groups of people occupying the same space, each focused on different projects. Groups work together to use the workspace to fit a variety of needs. Clearly, the old individual and traditional workspaces are passing from the scene.

2. Today's workers must have strong communication skills. *Listening* to others has never been more important than it is in today's business world.

3. Collaboration is also more vital than ever. The skills of each member must also adapt to be used in a team approach to achieving goals.

4. But independent work can be just as important as teamwork. Flexible thinking recognizes that every member needs private time for research, experimentation, further study or refinement, and other times of secluded work. Today, everyone must understand his or her strengths and know how, when, and from whom to seek collaborative work.

5.  Employers and employees must be flexible in the ways they work together. *Bending* to meet the needs of the workplace is essential to effective work.

6.  Personal and group reflection are drivers of effective work. A vital question always hangs in a healthy work atmosphere: "What value did I or we provide today?" That can lead to other questions: "How can we best continue to provide this value?" Or, "What must we do differently to provide that value to ourselves and others?"

As a teacher, I worked to make sure our flexible learning supported those points. Our classroom spaces must be adaptive and supportive, reflecting the ever-changing needs of students and their future workplaces.

We must measure flexible learning environments by how well they align with the experiences and skills learners will need when they leave public school to join the workforce. That's why I've always focused on making sure my classrooms gave students much more than a cool space. I knew the whole point was to help them prepare for the future they will be stepping into.

○ **TEACHER TIP:**
Track your journey as you transform your classroom. Take photos, keep documents, record important key moments. You never know when you'll need them. I was glad to have kept photos of my classrooms from so many years back. They helped provide a living legacy to share with others.

## Closing the Door One Last Time

May 24, 2019, the last day of school for our students, was also my final day of a thirty-three-year career. I walked out the classroom door, still loving what I had done for so long. On that last day, I felt like we had all floated through a slow-motion finale of high fives, hugs, cheers, and tears. I felt ready to enjoy my summer break, not retire! That particular room had been my home away from home for five years. But that day was not the first of my summer break; it was the first day of my new life. No more lesson preparations, papers to grade, or time with the people—students and colleagues—I loved to serve. No more parent-teacher conferences, hallway decorating, hamsters, or hot-air balloons.

I heard the familiar click as the door closed behind me for a final time. I smiled, content with my past and excited about my future of helping other teachers.

Using flexible seating in my classroom transformed my teaching. And as I look to my future as an educational consultant, I'll have many opportunities to support others as they transform their educational spaces, journeying on the high and worthy path.

○ **TEACHER TIP:**
Always remember the blessings your journey brought you. Never take anything for granted. The knowledge you have gained along the way can support another teaching colleague next week, next month, or into the future.

# Appendices

### Appendix A: Seating Expectations
A suggested guideline for proper usage of furniture in the learning space. We added photos to support the visual learner, and I kept wording to a minimum. You can create one similar to this for each learning area in the room and post them at the locations to serve as reminders.

### Appendix B: Lesson Plan Template
I developed this planning template to assist educators when mapping out a unit. Each symbol represents one of the components to a flexible classroom. The symbols allow educators to see every component and its frequency at a glance.

### Appendix C: Physical Room Arrangement Taxonomy
This appendix includes environment designs with diagrams and descriptions. These can be used to optimize learning experiences and increase engagement. The numbers of each design correlate with the numbers referenced in the planning template on pages 98 and 99.

### Appendix D: All Teacher Tips
This is the catchall place for my teacher tips. You can easily reference them here by topic.

## Appendix A: Seating Expectations

### To be the Best, above the Rest!
### Our Seating Expectations

TALL CHAIRS
- Only 1 person on a chair at a time
- No tipping
- All 4 chair legs on the ground
- Human feet hang off chair

SOFT SEATING
- Only 1 person on a chair at a time
- Feet on the floor
- No tipping

WOBBLE STOOLS
- Only 1 person on a chair at a time
- No tipping
- Rocking is terrific!
- Both human feet must be on the floor

## Appendix B: Lesson Plan Template

| Monday | Tuesday | Wednesday | Thursday | Friday |
|--------|---------|-----------|----------|--------|
|        |         |           |          |        |
|        |         |           |          |        |
|        |         |           |          |        |
|        |         |           |          |        |

◌ Teacher lesson: group or 1:1 support or extension. Students teaching others as well.

○ Physical Room Arrangement Taxonomy

◎ Assessment-Formal and Summative Assessment (entrance, exit tickets, quizzes, interviews, anecdotal records)

# Appendix C: Physical Room Arrangement Taxonomy

## 1 RETREAT BUNGALOWS

Niches spaced apart in room.

Students can spread out as they deem fit or be teacher-guided.

## 2 TRIADS, PAIRS, QUADS

Collaborative or cooperative work in small numbers.

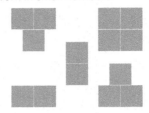

Experiments, smaller group tasks, focus groups, dissections or experiments, cocreating.

## 3 L-SHAPE

Pairs or quads support work, small group tasks, group reflections and problem-solving. Cooperative work.

## 4 HORSESHOE

Whole group observation, interaction with and around a central stage.

Presentations, debate or deliberations, theater.

## 5 FISHBOWL

Whole group observation, interaction with a central micro task demonstration or process.

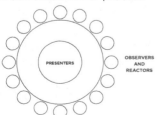

PRESENTERS

OBSERVERS AND REACTORS

Presentations, debate or deliberations, theater.

## 6 SPOKE

Whole group observation followed by smaller break-out clusters.

Exploration opportunities, expert presentation, collaborative or cooperative work.

| **7** FOUR CORNERS | **8** ARROW |
|---|---|
| Individual or small group.<br><br><br><br>Points of view. Presentation prep. Small-group tasks, breakout interest groups, teacher focus group support or extensions. Collaborative or cooperative work. | <br><br>Presentations, assessments, game challenges, manipulation, constructing and experimentation work. Cooperative work. |

| **9** PANEL | **10** FAN |
|---|---|
| 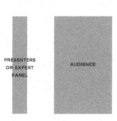<br><br>Deliberation, debate, points of view, expert presentation, media programs | <br><br>Interest-focused groups, experiments, teacher-focused less (in center or at each fan fold). |

| **11** MAZE | **12** WHOLE HUDDLE |
|---|---|
| <br><br>Whole class interactions. Student choice or teacher appointed. | 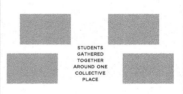<br><br>Grounding and preparation for an upcoming task, teacher or student-led whole-group lesson. Cooperative or collaborative work. |

## Appendix D: All Teacher Tips

### STARTING OUT

○ Be willing to chase your dreams when it comes to changing your classroom. If you feel the need to change things, then your students probably do, too. Don't get stuck in the mud with traditional approaches. Dare to dream.

○ Remember to bring uniqueness to your space when searching for treasures. Students will love you for the effort.

○ Remember that garage sales in the summer almost always include used furniture. You can snatch them up inexpensively for your classroom. Sometimes, if you explain why you want it, the owner will donate it to your classroom.

○ Consider asking your students' parents for gift cards to a particular store you've been eyeing a piece of furniture for the classroom. You might be surprised what they are eager to donate toward.

○ If you are not ready to implement free seating/learning all day, try it for one subject a week. Start small.

○ Remember, although the changes in your room will be exciting to most, it is okay if not everyone loves the changes. Keeping a foot in traditional while moving into the new is acceptable. It provides the grounding some students need to feel comfortable with changes.

○ It is often better for a teacher to listen more than he or she talks. Speaking less can be better when trying to understand students.

### CLASSROOM AMBIANCE AND SET-UP

○ Consider adding a fish tank to your room. It need not be a 150-gallon one. A fifteen-gallon freshwater tank would serve the purpose of introducing another species of life to spark student interests in something outside themselves.

- Consider adding one construction element to a unit you are teaching. Bring supplies from home, such as toilet paper rolls, string, toothpicks, or yarn. Have them handy for unique demonstrations of any topic.

- I believe every classroom space needs an anchor. Something as simple as tape marked on the floor to sit inside or around can serve as a common area. It doesn't have to be elaborate; it just needs to serve the purpose of bringing bodies and hearts together. Think of these areas as indoor patios.

- Asking your students for their reactions is the best golden nugget you can ever get. Their honesty will help you carry the classroom environment and its changes further than anyone else ever could. They are the clients of your work and matter most. Listen to them.

- Stop, look, and listen for unique and repurposed furniture as you pass through your community. You may be surprised at the new treasures and creative ideas that will come to you.

- Inexpensive and repurposed items can transform a space with little investment. The revised space will give students space to breathe, rest, and focus.

- Consider downsizing your teacher desk. It will provide more freedom for you than you realize. Doing so gives the students permission to downsize their supplies, too. Quite exhilarating!

- If a total downsizing of your teacher workspace seems too much, go small. Just change one section of your room at a time. Start by identifying what is essential. When you know that, ask if it must remain on your desk. Do you really need 1,000 markers, sticky notes, erasers, and note paper? Can you eliminate half the supplies? Could your teacher space hold only your computer, document camera, and one small bucket of pens? The freedom that comes to you through keeping things simple may surprise you.

- Supplies include teacher supplies, students' individual supplies, classroom common supplies, and specific learning tasks supplies. Think about which supplies are needed daily, weekly, or as a one-time necessity. Then create space for these items as you plan the use of the physical space.

○ Think outside the box about rhythms and routines. Is there anything small you can tweak to streamline your class routines? Roll call, supply collections?

○ Remember that whatever you create and optimize in your corner areas should be as stellar and valued as what's in the center of the classroom.

○ Consider adding a grow light with trays for seedlings, small plastic terrariums, or even an ant farm to your room. Live plants (or other inhabitants!) really do add dimension and wonder in the learning space.

○ Don't forget that classroom walls, doors, and floors also represent prime learning territory. They too should nudge students in the right direction. For example, inspiring and positive quotes on walls and doors nudge students into proper attitudes and thinking.

○ To add zest to your room, consider adding a signature piece of furniture or a wall piece. Make your room stand out as it sends a message of care and style to the students. Let them know that this shared space is so much more than any other classroom.

○ Ever consider painting a large "window" or mural on a wall? It can open the door to creativity! The wardrobe from the Narnia series would be a perfect backdrop in a literature-focused space!

○ Consider the instructional purpose and learner age/ grade to guide your thinking of wall use.

○ When placing boards on the wall, try hanging them in different directions or angles. Everything doesn't have to be parallel on the wall.

○ Today, many schools incorporate common spaces for a pod or cluster of classrooms. Think of these as extensions of the classroom; they are not just a space where kids can work quietly out of sight. These spaces are designed to allow greater student interaction. Think of the shared space as an opportunity to enrich the learning. Invite other grade levels or disciplines to interact there.

- The hallway should be an extension of the learning space. Mark off large squares outside the classroom door, calling them the "indoor patios." Students can reserve these spaces, moving foldable camp chairs or cushions to the spots. Provide fun and cheap lanterns or other related themed items for them in those areas. Learning is much more fun and inviting when what was once considered "the hallway" is now "the patio," "nook," or "garden." A small plant can rest inside each area. Create similar spaces outside as well, if available.

- Individual carpet squares can also define workspaces. Ask carpet stores for their outdated samples. Place them in key locations throughout the room. Students can grab one and work wherever they like.

- Think of the tasks students will be doing. Then make sure the room supports them through its physical layout and visual appeal.

- If you prefer a certain type of seating or table, try to add it to your classroom space. Whether a tractor stool, kitchen table, or unusual clipboards, adding something you love will influence your students as well. That makes learning more fun for everyone.

## STUDENT VOICE AND CHOICE

- Occasionally allow students to mix up their seating locations. Observe their reactions. Do they like the change? Does the change stimulate more excitement about learning?

- Give students a voice to address problems they see in the classroom. Maybe their thoughts will open conversations beyond the curriculum, just as the hot-air balloons did.

- As you think of students who may be less receptive to a flexible environment, consider how changes in the classroom can support them. Ask them to try out the new stool or desk. Help them see that their thoughts are valued. Simply showing that you value their opinion can provide the foundation of trust and respect they need. Sometimes that means they will champion a particular kind or piece of furniture. That's why my folding camp chairs were a much bigger hit than I had expected. I asked parents to purchase one or more chairs for the students and they willingly came through. Small asks can result in big results.

- It is okay if a particular student needs to sit in a particular chair and nowhere else in the room. Learn to give a bit with your students and you'll discover they will give more in return.

- Allow your students the opportunity to make little changes in their seating, for comfort. Even changing the direction their chair faces or turning it sideways to sit can make a more positive and friendly learner.

- Remember that the furnishings in the classroom are important to everyone. So, talk to your students about their preferences for seating and learning. When you do, you may find that giving them a voice is even more important than the furniture itself.

- Human beings aren't meant to stay stationery. Foot tapping, rocking gently back and forth, and wiggling can help anyone when they need to think. This is natural and should be allowed.

- When a change in the classroom isn't accepted as you hope, don't take it personally. Some classes don't mix well with unconventional furniture. Just store the piece in a closet until later in the month or year, when you can try it again. Students may just need time to adjust to the options.

- Your students' opinions the best golden nuggets you can get. Their honesty will help you carry the classroom environment and its changes further than anyone else ever could. They are the clients of your work and they matter most. Listen to them.

- Seating options are just that: options. Give grace when students suddenly decide the chair, stool, or pillow doesn't work. Let them shift. Making a big deal out of the little things will drive you and the students crazy;

they will feel you aren't honoring their learning needs, and they will be less willing to work. No one likes being strapped down in one seat all day.

○ The very act of offering seating options adds a spark to learning environments.

## CLASSROOM COMMUNITY

○ Morning Meetings are a great way to gather kids together to build community and cohesion in the classroom. All ages in K-12 need to be heard, seen, and understood as individuals. Those meetings can start small by getting to know each other's food, pet, hobby, sports, music, and movie preferences. The more we learn about each other, the more we can know and support each other.

○ How do you show your students you trust them? Find ways to allow freedom—like sitting somewhere different. Try it. Break some molds and traditions.

○ Too many times we think of classroom management as classroom discipline. These are not the same. Management means effective teacher instruction and, I believe, support of the learning environment. Students are part of this. Discipline is usually associated as a negative reaction to inappropriate behavior. Working together to achieve cohesiveness everyone in the learning environment can agree on is key. This creates a manageable and positive classroom environment.

○ It is important to document progress, challenges, and successes with every class project. Having some evidence of the learning for future generations grounds the experience but more importantly provides a voice for the students and their impact made in the school or community. You never know when a student may rise to become a world changer from a simple project in your class.

○ Document your journey as you transform your classroom. Take photos, keep documents, record important key moments. You never know when you'll need them. I was glad to have kept photos of my classrooms from so many years back. They helped provide a living legacy to share with others.

## CURRICULUM

○ Look closely at a unit you are going to teach. Explore the opportunities to change the layout of the room. Sometimes just moving a piece of furniture leads to paradigm shift. Try it!

○ Provide students with other simple handheld tools or device to help them work through stress or difficult work in the classroom. Items like stress balls or hour-glass timers give students opportunities to destress while working.

○ When planning projects for the class, think outside the box. As in the Beds for Barks unit, is there another community outreach that needs support? A local zoo or park needing bird houses?

○ Try planning one curricular unit a trimester or a month to start. I was always surprised at the level of excitement and love of learning that planning produces in students.

○ Releasing students to embrace a project that addresses authentic needs will elevate them and build an experience they will not forget.

○ Go big when looking for a unique partnership. Always remember there are others who hold the same desires your students feel. Research and reach out. You never know what might develop.

○ Whether you display your anchor charts the entire year or not, remember they serve the purpose of instruction and their clients are the students. If students can write and display their work on charts and create the how-tos, their learning goes much further than any fancy charts we create because students are taking the lead in their learning as they teach others.

○ Think of value related and life-giving field trip experiences. Arrange for students to visit a local nursery. They might even ask for a donation of small starter plants. Then give them the responsibility to care for them. Student groups can create plant journals. Each year a new team of botanists can continue a tradition that can build a legacy for future classes. They can even give the plants to local stores or senior centers as gifts if the students think that's a good idea. Begin with new starter plants the following year.

○ Always remember the blessings your journey brought you. Never take anything for granted. The knowledge you have gained from it can support another teaching colleague next week, next month, or at other points in the future.

## Endnotes

1.  Emelina Minero, "Flexible Seating Elevates Student Engagement." Edutopia. August 4, 2015. https://www.edutopia.org/practice/flexible-classrooms-providing-learning-environment-kids-need.

2.  Rex Miller, et al., *Change Your Space, Change Your Culture: How Engaging Workspaces Lead to Transformation and Growth* (Hoboken, NJ: Wiley, 2014).

3.  Although generally acknowledged throughout academic journals and leaders, the idea of the "4 C's" as presented probably originated with *The Partnership for 21st Century Skills*.

4.  This podium, from MeTEOR Education, brought me a sense of clutter relief.

5.  Rex Miller, *The Healthy Workplace Nudge: How Healthy People, Culture, and Buildings Lead to High Performance* (Hoboken, NJ: John Wiley and Sons, 2018).

6.  Ibid., 127.

7.  Rex Miller, Bill Latham, Kevin Baird, and Michelle Kinder, *WHOLE: What Teachers Need to Help Students Thrive* (Hoboken, NJ: Jossey-Bass, 2020).

8.  David Thornburg, *From the Campfire to the Holodeck: Creating Engaging and Powerful 21st Century Environments* (San Francisco, CA: Jossey-Bass, 2014).

## About the Author

Kelly Almer is a lifelong teacher and learner. Having retired from classroom teaching, she now coaches other teachers. And with this book, she is now an author. For Kelly, writing is as natural as watching Hallmark movies at Christmas with a cup of chai tea.

Kelly grew up in Colorado and it will always be her home. She has always had a passion for teaching and coaching others, and especially for helping others to see the benefits of flexible learning environments.

She taught fourth, fifth, sixth, and seventh grades, gifted and talented classes, and technology. She also served as an instructional coach.

Teaching was not Kelly's first love; as a child she wanted to be an artist. But she graduated with her degree in elementary education in 1984 and then earned her master of arts degree in administration, supervision, and curriculum development in 1992. She has since earned an additional ninety semester hours in educational coursework to further her teaching craft.

Kelly has written and received over fifteen grants to benefit her students. She won a national contest from Compaq computers for an innovative cross-country social studies unit. She has been a presenter at ITSE and InnEdCO multiple times. Kelly served on her district's science and language arts councils, was nominated for the Disney Teacher of the Year Award, and was a member of her district's teacher support team. She has also continued her art, creating watercolor paintings of wedding bouquets and wedding crests for the brides who carry them. But her crowning achievement is teaching over 1,500 students ranging in age from kindergartners to seventh graders.

When Kelly isn't coaching, you can find her reading the latest *New York Times* bestseller, painting in her studio, or taking walks with her husband and two grown kids through their lovely Colorado community.

## Acknowledgements

This book has taken me thirty-three years to write. And I am indebted to many who helped along my path. I regret that I cannot name them all, but I must thank those most pivotal to this book.

I thank the many outstanding administrators and colleagues who supported and encouraged my dreams. You also helped me to refine my teaching craft.

I thank those who were my beta readers—Cathy Putman, Cherie Haskett, Jana Webb, and Abby McArthy. Without your honest feedback, this book wouldn't be what it is today. Thank you for seeing things I couldn't and for pushing me to expand my horizons for the betterment of all educators.

To Bill Latham of MeTEOR Education, thank you for your interest in my manuscript. You not only believed in the merits of my story, but you gave my voice a megaphone. You made my writing journey a path worth taking.

To my editor, Ed Chinn, thank you for finding my heartstrings and voice. I couldn't have done this without you.

Mom and Dad, you have both been pillars throughout my life. I love you both for encouraging my dreams and talents. Thank you for your unconditional love. Love you always.

To my sister, Kim, and our brother, Kevin. I'll always remember our adventures growing up together and I'm grateful you are both in my life. I love you both.

To my children, Caitlin and Steven. You have both given great joy to me and to our home. And you have both given me and your dad the gift of lives made richer and filled with love more than we could imagine. You dare to make your dreams happen. Love you to the moon, beyond, and back.

To my husband, Mark, thank you for supporting me, my dreams, and my ambitions. You have always done whatever you could to help me accomplish them. You built things for my classrooms and even purchased a turkey dinner for the family of one of my students who could not afford it. I think in your heart, my students were your students, too. I love you forever and am so grateful we are on the same life journey together.